MY POCKET
TAI CHI

MY POCKET
TAI CHI

Improve Focus. Reduce Stress. Find Balance.

ADAMS MEDIA

NEW YORK LONDON TORONTO SYDNEY NEW DELHI

Adams Media
An Imprint of Simon & Schuster, Inc.
57 Littlefield Street
Avon, Massachusetts 02322

First Adams Media trade paperback edition MAY 2018

ADAMS MEDIA and colophon are trademarks of Simon and Schuster.

For information about special discounts for bulk purchases, please contact Simon & Schuster Special Sales at 1-866-506-1949 or business@simonandschuster.com.

The Simon & Schuster Speakers Bureau can bring authors to your live event. For more information or to book an event contact the Simon & Schuster Speakers Bureau at 1-866-248-3049 or visit our website at www.simonspeakers.com.

Interior design by Colleen Cunningham
Interior illustrations by Eric Andrews

Manufactured in China

10 9 8 7 6 5 4 3 2 1

Library of Congress Cataloging-in-Publication Data has been applied for.

ISBN 978-1-5072-0724-6
ISBN 978-1-5072-0725-3 (ebook)

Contains material adapted from the following title published by Adams Media, an Imprint of Simon & Schuster, Inc.: *The Everything® Tai Chi and QiGong Book* by Ellae Elinwood, copyright © 2002, ISBN 978-1-58062-646-0.

CONTENTS

INTRODUCTION **9**

WHAT IS TAI CHI? 10

TRACING TAI CHI'S ROOTS 11

CHOOSING AMONG THE FOUR BRANCHES OF TAI CHI 13

TAI CHI IS A MOVEMENT PHILOSOPHY 14

PART 1: THE BENEFITS OF TAI CHI / 15

CHAPTER 1: BODY **17**

HELPS YOU BREATHE MORE EFFECTIVELY 18

IMPROVES YOUR COORDINATION AND BALANCE 23

STRAIGHTENS YOUR POSTURE 25

EXPANDS YOUR JOINT FLEXIBILITY 26

STRENGTHENS YOUR MUSCLES 26

GIVES YOU A HEALTHIER SKIN TONE 26

LOWERS YOUR BLOOD PRESSURE 27

PROVIDES RELIEF FROM MIGRAINES 28

CHAPTER 2: MIND **29**

REDUCES YOUR STRESS LEVELS 30

INTRODUCES YOU TO MOVING MEDITATION 30

IMPROVES YOUR ABILITY TO FOCUS 33

RELIEVES SOME SYMPTOMS OF DEPRESSION .34

HELPS YOU CLEAR YOUR MIND 34

TEACHES YOU TO SLOW DOWN 36

HARMONIZES YOUR MIND AND BODY 37

HARMONIZES YOUR BODY AND SOUL 40

CHAPTER 3: SPIRIT **43**

STRENGTHENS YOUR SPIRITUAL CONNECTION 44

HELPS YOU EMBRACE WU CHI, OR THE SOURCE OF ALL 45

TEACHES YOU TO BALANCE YOUR CHI 46

EMPHASIZES POSITIVE ENERGY 50

OFFERS A CONNECTION TO NATURE 51

IMPROVES YOUR RESILIENCY 57

PART 2: TAI CHI BASICS / 59

CHAPTER 4: PREPARING YOURSELF TO PRACTICE **61**

CREATING A SPACE 62

FINDING PROPER CLOTHING 63

READYING YOUR MIND 64

READYING YOUR BODY 67

CONSIDERING A CLASS OR TEACHER 69

ADOPTING A LEARNER'S ATTITUDE 74

TROUBLESHOOTING COMMON ISSUES 77

BASIC TAI CHI PRINCIPLES 79

CHAPTER 5: WARM UP **81**

CROSS CRAWL 82

CROSS CRAWL WITH TWIST 83

INFINITY ARMS 84

SHOULDER ROLLS 86

HULA PELVIS 87

SEXY PELVIS 87

FOOT FIGURE EIGHT 88

WRIST SWIRLS 90

ANKLE SWIRLS 91

ELBOW MASSAGE 92

PLIÉ 94

CHAPTER 6: STRETCHING **97**

SIDE STRETCH 98

NECK STRETCH 99

SUN SALUTATION 101

ANKLES 116

CHAPTER 7: BASIC STANCES **117**

FEET, LEGS, AND PELVIS SHAPE 118

50/50 POSTURE 122

70/30 POSTURE 123

100 PERCENT BACK 124

EMPTY FOOT ON HEEL 125

EMPTY FOOT ON TOE 126

STEPPING 127

90 DEGREES STEPPING 130

CHAPTER 8: HAND AND ARM POSTURES **133**

BEAUTIFUL LADY'S WRIST. 134

PALMS RESTING ON PILLOW OF AIR 135

SHOULDER DOWN TO ELBOW UP TO WRIST. 136

HOLDING THE BALL 137

WARD OFF 138

TWO-HANDED PUSH 139

ONE-HANDED PUSH. 140

HOOK HAND 141

FIST 142

MOVING ON TO THE YANG STYLE SHORT FORM. 143

CHAPTER 9: CONTINUING YOUR PRACTICE **145**

PRACTICING TAI CHI REGULARLY 146

BEING CONSISTENT 148

TAKING TAI CHI BREAKS 149

MAKING A COMMITMENT TO AN EXPANDED LIFE. 151

RESOURCES **153**

BOOKS 153

WEBSITES. 153

INDEX **155**

INTRODUCTION

Tai chi is an ancient movement activity that can help you reduce stress, improve your health, and relax your body. These simple, flowing activities were almost unknown in the Western world until the 1950s, but today they are popular worldwide...and with good reason! Tai chi can contribute greatly to your physical, mental, emotional, and spiritual well-being by improving your muscle tone, quieting your mind, and connecting you to your spiritual side, to name just a few benefits.

One additional benefit of tai chi is that, just like the best things in life, it's free. You don't need an expensive gym, trendy clothes, or special equipment—you can do these activities anywhere, anytime. Another plus is that because tai chi involves gentle, nonforceful movements, it's perfect for all ages and ability levels.

What Does Tai Chi Chuan Mean?

The words *tai chi chuan* are pronounced "tie chee chewan." They come to us from the book *I Ching*, which embodies the Chinese philosophy and faith of Taoism. (The Taoist philosophy was expressed by famed Chinese philosopher Lao Tzu in his book the *Tao Te Ching*.) *Tai chi* means "supreme ultimate." In the beginning of all things, there is oneness, and then the oneness divides into two forces—the female force of yin and the male force of yang. Tai chi is located in the nanosecond of the division of yin and yang. *Chuan* means "fisted hand." So *tai chi chuan* means "supreme ultimate fisted hand." (The "chuan" is now dropped because the "fist" portion of the term is rarely the focus.)

WHAT IS TAI CHI?

Tai chi (pronounced "tie chee" and sometimes spelled taiji) involves a series of prescribed positions done in predictable, flowing sequences that use every muscle and joint in the body. These flowing sequences are slow, relaxed, stylized, and comfortable motions that look a bit like swimming without the water. By gently twisting and turning as you balance and rebalance your arms and legs in a lovely, nonhurried, steady, flowing sequence, every portion of the body is used, refreshed, and revitalized.

When you see tai chi practiced for the first time, what will likely catch your attention is the grace, poise, and serenity emanating from the practitioner. That is how tai chi looks from the outside. To the person doing the movements, it is a calming, centering, and quieting experience that improves feelings of personal well-being and general health.

Tai chi chuan was developed by ancient Chinese monk-warriors as a martial art. In that time, the spiritual development of many monks was combined with the warrior's path. The goal was to have a peaceful inner world connected to the oneness of life and also to have tremendous martial arts skills. Perfection was achieved by maintaining peace and honing warrior skills at the same time.

The practice of tai chi chuan began somewhere between 550 B.C. and A.D. 1300. Tai chi chuan was taught and transmitted through the centuries in secrecy. The teaching was passed from master to student in the strictest of privacy. For centuries, the secrets of tai chi chuan were well guarded among a privileged few, but sometime around the late 1800s or early 1900s it was exposed to the Chinese general public.

TRACING TAI CHI'S ROOTS

The earliest references to tai chi chuan involve a Chinese hermit named Xu Xuan Ping, who some say formed the basis for tai chi with his thirty-seven patterns of movement. The patterns were also referred to as Changquan (Long Fist), after Long River (the nickname of the Yangtze River), because the movements of tai chi chuan were reminiscent of a river—flowing, powerful, and uninterrupted. Very close to the same time, Li Dao Zi, a Taoist priest, practiced a similar physical movement. These first emergences of tai chi occurred during the Tang dynasty (A.D. 618–907).

Tai Chi's Connection to Martial Arts

Martial arts in the ancient world didn't simply mean self-defense, but was a way of life for monks who were also warriors, and described the revered balance of Old China. Tai chi without the chuan (fisted hand) is enjoyed by many people today as a tool for better health, longevity, and improved well-being. These very qualities contributed to a more balanced life for a warrior-monk and also enhanced his fighting skills. Harmony, a calm attitude, and receptivity to increased mental clarity became aspects of martial arts to which warriors aspired. The warrior was able to blend this embodied art of inner harmony with the outer force of battle—to be in a warrior's conflict, conducting the business of war, but still filled with inner peace. They were in the midst of life while in the midst of death. It was from this need that tai chi chuan (which is today's tai chi coupled with martial arts) was born.

The term "tai chi chuan" was probably first referenced in the writings of Chen Ling Xi's *The Method to Attain Enlightenment Through Observing the Scripture*. It was at this time that tai chi chuan seems to have been blended into the monk-warrior traditions by men who were skillful in martial arts practice and spiritual development. It was then through the skills and observations of the priest Zhang San Feng that tai chi chuan came into full prominence. Zhang San Feng was a great master teacher who happened upon a fight between a snake and some type of bird (some references say a crane; others, a sparrow). As the bird struck, the snake would avoid contact by using graceful, serpentine movements, waiting and swaying until it was ready to accurately strike. Watching this forceful but graceful combat, he was inspired to take what he had learned from observing the wisdom of nature and apply it to his own martial arts. His style (called Shaolin Kungfu) had been more forceful, but it took on more graceful mannerisms after his life-changing experience in nature. He called it Wudang 32-Pattern Long Fist, which developed into tai chi chuan as we know it today.

Tai Chi's Connection to the *I Ching*

The words *tai chi* come originally from the *I Ching*. The *I Ching* has been called many things—an oracle, a guide, and a reflection of one's unconscious are a few. It is a wonderful book that imparts reflections on the action and interaction of yin and yang in the seeker's life. The *I Ching* continues to stand as a book of great philosophical value worldwide and is relevant to tai chi because it takes a deeper look at the forces of yin and yang in life events. You may want to read it in order to cultivate chi, balance yin and yang, and grace your life with the movements of tai chi.

The training continued to be passed to secular masters and disciples throughout China, but one theory holds it was probably a practitioner named Wang Zong Yue who taught the art to the powerful Chen family at their family settlement. It was through the Chen family, who claimed they learned it in the 1600s from their own ancestor Chen Wang Ting, that the Chen Style of tai chi chuan took form and spread. It was the contributions of this family that rooted the destiny of tai chi chuan. Yang Lu Chen (1799–1872) built the foundation of the Yang Style of tai chi chuan.

CHOOSING AMONG THE FOUR BRANCHES OF TAI CHI

There are currently four different branches of the tree of tai chi chuan. Each form has its own unique value:

1. The Wu Style emphasizes small movement and body technique for combat.
2. The Sun Style emphasizes high patterns and agile movements.
3. The Chen Style emphasizes the hard and fast.
4. The Yang Style emphasizes gentle, graceful movements for health.

Yang Style is the commonly taught form in the Western world and is, therefore, the form on which this book focuses. The Yang Style enlarges and smooths the movements that emphasize the graceful aspects of tai chi chuan. For this reason, it is sometimes called the Big Form. Yang Style has no foot stomping, punches, and so on. It is a pattern of slow, graceful movements that transforms tai chi chuan from a forceful martial art to the gentle health exercise of tai chi.

TAI CHI IS A MOVEMENT PHILOSOPHY

Tai chi is not a religion. It is a movement that has been evolving over centuries. Tai chi movement engages the practitioner's body, mind, and spirit in a great wholeness, oneness, or nothingness (called wu chi) as it divides tai chi—the energy moment—into yin and yang energy flows. It is for this reason that tai chi supports any faith or belief system.

Anytime Is the Right Time

Tai chi's philosophy can be taken up at any life stage or situation. You don't need to become stronger, improve your flexibility, drop some weight, or improve your health before you can start. You can start right now. Even if you have only partial movement, move what you can. Let it work for you now, as you are.

In this book you'll discover the wonderful benefits of tai chi, demonstrated in clear illustrations and simple, easy-to-follow instructions. Get ready to ditch the knots in your shoulders, clear your mind of worries, and find inner peace, one stance at a time.

PART 1

THE BENEFITS
OF TAI CHI

CHAPTER 1

BODY

Tai chi is amazingly beneficial to your body, from head to toe. Its emphasis on proper breathing can be life-changing in itself, plus you'll also enjoy better balance and coordination from tai chi's slow, thoughtful movements.

HELPS YOU BREATHE MORE EFFECTIVELY

We usually think of air as being empty, but in tai chi air is a full—even viscous—environment filled with a field of energy that connects us to the larger field of energy we call the universe. *Chi* is spirited vitality (or energy) from the universe—wholeness or nothingness. Chi travels in electric currents that fill the air around you. On these currents of chi is our life force. Without it, we die. When shallow breathing causes it to diminish, you are less lively, and this usually registers as stress. Repeated shallow breathing only perpetuates the stress you feel throughout your body—tight muscles, headaches and other pains, and difficulty focusing.

Breathing Is Vital to Health

Improved breathing improves your overall health. Deeper and larger breaths bring more oxygen into the blood. The body also goes through a natural exercise when inhaling deeply. Your chest expands and lifts, the lungs expand, the torso lengthens, the organs move a bit, the hips expand slightly, the spine lengthens, and even the bony plates of your skull expand somewhat. Our bodies were built to have this exercise several times a minute for our entire lives. We can all stop and take a deep breath when we think about it, but that may not be very often. Tai chi teaches you how to develop deep, relaxed breathing so effectively that your body is reminded to breathe deeply. If your body is fully reminded and indulged in this breathing, it will create a way to continue the experience. Just as your body notifies you about thirst and hunger, it will do the same with breathing. After all, we can go much longer without either food or water than we can without air, so air is your first priority for being relaxed. It would be impossible to feel relaxed with a bare minimum of food or a few sips of water. Who knows how much stress we all carry just as a result of poor breathing! Let tai chi help you breathe more completely. Perhaps it will help you resolve any breathing problems you may have.

The Importance of Breathing Exercises

Just as breath is stored in the lungs, chi is stored in the *tan t'ien*, a place located in the deep center of the pelvis about 1⅓ inches below the navel. All breath work is designed to fill, store, and finally cultivate chi in the tan t'ien. For this reason, all the breath exercises carry as their single purpose the goal of gaining control over your chi.

Because tai chi moves every joint, it promotes optimum circulation of blood and oxygen throughout the body. In order to have optimum health and well-being, you must create an inner environment where the chi can penetrate even the most resistant spot. These areas that would not ordinarily have an abundance of chi are the areas that become most vulnerable to injury and disease.

How to Breathe Properly

Tai chi is based on your most natural breathing. Slow, gentle, and deep, it increases lung capacity and expands the organs so that oxygen fills the body on the inhale. When you exhale, carbon dioxide exits, freeing the body of waste products.

Make Tai Chi Breathing
Part of Your Day

To get your body back in balance during a stressful day, take a minute and do some tai chi breathing. A few moments will settle you down. Because of your body's muscle memory, the more frequently you interject tai chi breathing into your day, the more quickly and effectively you will feel the effects.

Unless otherwise instructed, breathe in through your nose, but call your breath into the body through the tan t'ien, not the nose. Then bring it down to the perineum, up the spine, and out the nose on the exhale while the chi flows down the front in the tan t'ien. If the tan t'ien is not involved, which means you expand the lower lungs and abdomen out on the inhale and in on the exhale, then your breath will be shallow in the lungs and your chest will be tense. Your body then loses its natural center of gravity. This is one of the most common reasons for tension and the fatigue that results. Many people find that when they start tai chi, their need for sleep diminishes naturally: they either stay up longer or get up earlier. Either way, people practicing tai chi feel refreshed after sleep, and this feeling of being well-rested stays with them throughout the day. The reason for this is simple: because of the natural orientation of tai chi, the body has the oxygen and chi it needs to run smoothly and effectively.

What Is Tan T'ien?

Deep in the center of the belly 1⅓ inches below the navel, tan t'ien is a place for centering yourself and is a gathering place for chi.

Try Reverse Breathing

Reverse breathing is an especially valuable breathing style. When used during the day along with just plain-old regular breathing, a nice development of breath and chi occurs. It's called reverse breathing because you ask your body to do the opposite of what it would instinctively do.

To try reverse breathing, simply reverse the natural, relaxed breath. Take a deep breath and as you inhale, pull or contract your stomach muscles in and up. Now exhale and extend these same stomach muscles down and out. This breathing technique requires attention, for as soon as your attention slips, you will return to normal breathing.

To further engage the rejuvenating aspects of reverse breathing, you can use two words that ancients used during breathing. Because of the power of the words in conjunction with the breath, it is suggested that they first be incorporated into normal breathing. Say "heng" as you inhale, and "ha" as you exhale.

Including Intent

Your intent can move the chi from the outside to the inside of your body and also from the inside to the outside. Intent means imagining the chi moving from outside to inside and then back again—the chi will follow your mental command.

You can also combine intent with movement. For example, as you inhale, lift and open your arms to send your chi in and out of your body. Exhale and let your arms relax to your sides.

Renew Yourself with Reverse Breathing

Use reverse breathing when you're feeling stressed, have low energy, are waiting in line or for someone to arrive, feel depleted, still have a lot more of the day left and the day is demanding, or any time you're able to take a few minutes to renew yourself.

Staying Relaxed As You Breathe

The main principle for any breathing exercise is to be as relaxed as possible. Use your mind to direct the breath and chi. For example, imagine that your breath is not only going into your lungs but is also going into your shoulders, hips, any place that hurts, and so on. This is known as directing the chi. Many people actually begin to feel that the breath is going into other areas of the body as well as into the lungs.

Freely Moving Chi

After you've relaxed, your body will be in an open and comfortable position. At this time, chi starts freely moving throughout the body. It is this freely circulating chi that provides more energy and oxygen than is found in those who do not avail themselves of these skills.

If you're standing, imagine your legs solidly under you, filled with great strength. When you start the breath/movement, move slowly and cultivate the feeling of stability in your legs. Never go too fast, too far, or do too much. Be regular in your practice, as regular as you are with brushing your teeth. Daily movements or standing meditations create an inner environment for developing a substantial increase in your internal power. They show the body what to relax and how to relax it. The areas of the body that are tense become obvious to you: they become twitchy, achy, and generally uncomfortable. Relief comes only through pursuing mental, emotional, and physical relaxation as a part of the standing meditation.

As you do tai chi exercises, you will find no oxygen deficit. You should experience no shortness of breath, no trying to catch your breath, and no taking time out to get your breath in order to continue. Tai chi is different from other exercises because it actually regulates oxygen consumption and keeps pace with your body's oxygen needs. Most other exercises put you into oxygen debt (which is what happens when activated muscles demand more oxygen than is being received). Tai chi, when taught well, never creates this situation. Allow tai chi to open the ligaments, strengthen the muscles, and improve your breath as it has been designed to do.

Daily Breathing Checklist

Have you:

- Allowed natural breath?
- Relaxed your abdomen?
- Taken a slow, deep inhale?
- Relaxed and just let the exhale go on its own?
- Remembered to do the reverse breathing?
- Gently placed your fingers on the tan t'ien?

IMPROVES YOUR COORDINATION AND BALANCE

Balanced strength and improved coordination occur because the tai chi positions incorporate all the muscles of the body appropriately, and the muscles strengthen in natural balance with one another. They give support to one another as they were designed by nature to do. Their elasticity returns. Because you're working your body as it was meant to be worked—completely, thoroughly, and fluidly—the body relearns how to move without injury and remembers how to move with graceful coordination.

Eastern traditions focus on creating coordination—through strength and flexibility—throughout the body. In ancient China great battles were waged between districts, clans, and families (and even within families), and so the need for effective self-protection was ever present. One had to fight with strength and suppleness to win. As the culture chose civilization over warring, these self-protection arts were improved into systems of martial arts. Then, as the martial arts became more refined, the disciplines became more intricate and sophisticated. One need only to look at an accomplished tai chi practitioner or martial artist to see these principles in action. In the beginning you may not leap in the air and land silently like a cat, but you will find your walk and movements more graceful and your strength increasing.

How Much Does Tai Chi Cost?

Because no special equipment is required and the information about the sequenced motions is readily available, there is precious little required to start. Your only expense will be for the method of instruction you choose: a video (about $30, or free if you find something reputable on *YouTube*), a private class (about $60), or a group class (about $25). Of course, you can make it as expensive as you choose with special (but not truly necessary) clothes and shoes, trips to tai chi intensive camps, and subscriptions to magazines and book clubs. But these are all extras. Even though they add variety and enhance learning, they are not in the least essential for the initial learning and practice of your own tai chi activity.

You may think that standing balance—on your feet, gazing forward—would be the easiest thing in the world. It is actually not easy to simply stand in one place, unmoving, balanced between earth and heaven. This is usually a structural/muscular problem. Not only do we shorten our breath as we become adults, we also contort, to varying degrees, our body. Injuries, accidents, and prolonged stress all lay claim to throwing off the natural, easy balance we had as children. We don't arrive at unsteadiness in an instant. Poor balance develops over time as the injuries, accidents, and stress continue to hold the body in misalignment. Healing from an injury or an accident doesn't in any way mean you will get your body back the way it was before. Those injured areas may be stiffer after they have completely healed. Stress builds upon itself, creating an unpleasant cycle of increasing stiffness and a slow, degenerating balance. Tai chi, one muscle at a time, one joint at a time, brings your body back to balance.

STRAIGHTENS YOUR POSTURE

Good posture allows your body to move properly. It also allows excellent blood circulation and great breathing. Over time, life can bow you. Work positions (sitting slumped over a computer) and everyday life takes a toll on how straight and confidently you stand.

Tai chi places great importance on the spine. The head should balance delicately on the spine. The movements initiate at the tan t'ien so that the pelvis (or as the ancients spoke of it, the waist) can be supple and freely moving. The natural result of these principles is that your posture straightens and your movements become more graceful and easy. Good posture is a statement of mechanical efficiency. It is an eloquent statement of tai chi's effectiveness!

Tai chi also improves your spinal health, which helps your posture. Loosened hip joints and legs provide a stable, balanced foundation. The spine is the superhighway on which the chi runs. Connected to other energy centers in the body, the spine is where the chi courses to its destinations. A flexible, agile, and free spine is essential for the resiliency of good health and well-being to enter your body, mind, and spirit. Ideally, you want your spine to move like a flexible cord, able to twist side to side, bend over easily, and roll up from a bent position with comfort. When loosening your spine, don't force it; instead, give it time to find its flexible comfort. For breathing practice, imagine that you're breathing down the front of your spine when you inhale and that your breath is circulating up the back of your spine as you exhale. Tai chi allows you to loosen your spine as well as your hip joints for good posture.

EXPANDS YOUR JOINT FLEXIBILITY

Many people have stiff joints, whether from repetitive strain, age, or old injuries. Tai chi practice makes your joints more flexible. The simple poses and gentle stretches are safe and effective ways to loosen joints. You'll feel less pain, experience less stiffness—all while learning a new skill! Tai chi is a great way to heal after a joint injury such as a broken ankle or a hip replacement—talk to your doctor about when you can begin practice.

STRENGTHENS YOUR MUSCLES

In the Western world, when we think of strength we often think of people who want to bulk up their large muscles, usually through weight lifting. However, strength means a variety of things. Strength can also mean being strong in your favorite sport. Strength can also mean paying attention to your muscles, not to bulk up but to stay fit and healthy. The postures and movements in tai chi will help you strengthen both your major and secondary muscle groups.

GIVES YOU A HEALTHIER SKIN TONE

Your skin glows when you regularly practice tai chi. Why? This is because tai chi:

* Improves circulation
* Reduces stress (which is responsible for early body aging)
* Boosts and balances those chi pathways throughout the body

No matter what your skin type, the texture of your skin will likely improve as you practice tai chi. Skin problems that occur in adolescence and prior to menstruation can sometimes be positively affected with the practice of tai chi because of the rebalancing going on deep within the body. Your organs will function better, and this shows immediately in the skin. In addition the deep breathing you practice during tai chi is wonderful for the tone, texture, and color of your skin.

Tai Chi and Pregnancy

Check with your doctor first to be sure your usual tai chi practice is still recommended for your personal health profile during pregnancy. Usually, because the normal tai chi movements are already gentle, you can continue your tai chi practice with very few changes. As your belly gets bigger you will have to accommodate somewhat, but not enough to diminish the positive gifts of tai chi.

LOWERS YOUR BLOOD PRESSURE

Hypertension (high blood pressure) can cause deadly strokes. Many tai chi practitioners have reduced their blood pressure or lowered the amount of medication they need to control their condition thanks to the gentle exercise and careful attention they pay to their body. If you have high blood pressure, check with your doctor about your exercise program and take your blood pressure readings frequently.

PROVIDES RELIEF FROM MIGRAINES

After a few months of tai chi practice, migraine sufferers may find a reduction in their painful symptoms. One reason may be the effects tai chi has on circulation and its ability to help quiet heightened nerve responses to life's challenges. One remedy for migraine sufferers is to try to prevent blood from engorging in the brain and instead force it to be released into the arms and legs, which are often cold during a migraine attack. Tai chi balances circulation.

Migraines often occur in people who are quiet and sensitive by nature. The constant barrage of sounds and sights in this world can be overstimulating to even the most centered, mindful person. Tai chi provides a calm, peaceful outlet from everyday hustle and bustle. Just letting this type of relaxation take hold at regular intervals allows the downward flow of chi to have more movement. Whatever may happen to create the reduced symptoms is a blessing to anyone who has put up with the pain, nausea, and light sensitivity of migraines.

CHAPTER 2

MIND

Tai chi includes your mind in all its movements and helps you unify your body and mind. By-products of this connection include less stress, better focus, and an introduction into movement meditation.

REDUCES YOUR STRESS LEVELS

The tenets of tai chi lend themselves well to stress reduction. Quieting your busy mind, focusing on gentle arm movements, and remembering your posture and breathing all help melt away stress.

As you do tai chi, your overall focus will be to relax into your body. You should feel a release down into your hip joints and pelvis. When the hip joints are loosened and the pelvis is relaxed, then you can keep the lower body firm and stable and your feet grounded. There is also an emphasis on having the body rebalanced so that the bottom is heavy and the top is light. We usually hold a great deal of tension in the hip joints and tend to contract the pelvis. This tension and contraction creates a situation where it becomes impossible for the chi to sink into the tan t'ien. Tai chi emphasizes relaxing into the body and dropping the breath and chi into the tan t'ien.

INTRODUCES YOU TO MOVING MEDITATION

If you're interested in meditation but have trouble with the traditional "sitting still" method, try tai chi! Moving meditation is just what it sounds like: the person moves while meditating. The movement assists in maintaining a meditative state of mind. One style of this meditation is a walking meditation. In this style, the breath is coordinated with the movement of walking as the eyes remain in an unstrained and even gaze, blinking softly. The focus of the mind and thoughts is more fully on the movements of the body. The body relaxes more deeply into the familiar movement of walking. As a result of this increasing relaxation, the breath/chi moves more fully into the body on ever deepening breaths. This mind/thought/body/chi/breath union creates an environment of awareness in which the practitioner becomes more and more relaxed, receptive, and alive to the present moment—not relaxed and receptive in the sense of being like a zombie, but in the sense that all the exquisite, finely tuned aspects of life become more clear, more precious, and much more varied. Tai chi lends itself well to moving meditation because its movements are gentle but deliberate.

This ability to live in the present moment allows the emergence of your true nature as your habitual nature recedes. The habitual nature is the one you have developed over years of coping with life's stresses and difficult lessons. It is this habitual nature that denies your true nature the opportunity to engage life as a beautiful treasure. The habitual nature negotiates with life, always struggling in some way with fear. All meditation techniques are crafted to bring the true nature forward as the habitual nature recedes. A meditation may be performed either sitting or moving, but the intent is always to become more present by harmonizing the body, mind, and chi.

Tenets of Moving Meditation

Meditation makes your mind supreme over the body. For movement meditation, do the following:

1. Relax
2. Know emptiness and fullness
3. Have slowness and evenness
4. Balance
5. Root and sink
6. Breathe
7. Concentrate

Movement meditation is perfect for anyone who likes to move, is task oriented, and gets bored easily. The moving aspects can offset the restlessness that occurs from these personality characteristics. It is often much easier for an action-oriented person to master meditation in movement. The sitting aspects of meditation can be very unrewarding. Each type of meditation has equal value. Find the one that works for you. And as long as you are doing tai chi, the movement aspects of meditation will be a part of your life.

If you learn tai chi and continue to practice regularly, even daily, you will experience the gifts of movement meditation: feeling as though more time is available, being relaxed, breathing easier, and feeling happier. Instead of leaping in with your first response and then later having second thoughts, you have time to make decisions. Meditation in movement with tai chi helps you create an environment where time becomes more spacious. Life doesn't slow down, there is just more space between events.

Understanding the Seven Basic Meditation Practices

You can find many different forms and techniques of meditation, and all are aimed at the same goal—enlightenment. Enlightenment is defined as attainment of spiritual light. These various techniques are broken down into distinct types of meditation, and each one provides a different path to the same eventual outcome. Because people vary so much, these technique variations allow everyone to find meditation practices that they are comfortable with. The seven basic meditation practices are:

* Meditation through breathing exercises
* Meditation by concentrating one's thoughts on one point
* Meditation through visualization (art, music, mandalas)
* Meditation through mantra yoga (reciting certain words)
* Meditation by absorbing one's mind in goodwill or devotional thoughts

* Meditation by identifying the mind essence
* Meditation through movement and philosophies (yoga, tai chi, dance)

Mixing Meditation and Prayer

Meditation and some types of prayer are essentially the same. Some prayers acknowledge the greatness of a higher power; others thank that power for life and gifts; still others ask for intercession in personal or life events.

Another aspect of prayer is the entering into spiritual communion. It is this later form that has the same focus as meditation. Some sitting practices involve specific hand positions, some use chanting, and some use mantras.

A mantra is a simple, powerful phrase repeated over and over throughout the meditation. The words of the mantra are considered to be of great importance. For example, the phrase "om mani padme hum" is an essential mantra of Tibetan Buddhism. In Western traditions, an essential prayer might be "I am love." These mantras and prayers can be repeated silently with an inner voice as the practitioner goes through daily life.

IMPROVES YOUR ABILITY TO FOCUS

The ability to focus is perhaps one of the greatest gifts people seek from tai chi. The digital age has changed the world as we have known it. Everyone needs to balance in-person interactions, the stimulation of digital devices, and the constant onslaught of various media. Tai chi focuses your mind and improves your concentration by closing out distractions and bringing your mind to the present moment.

RELIEVES SOME SYMPTOMS OF DEPRESSION

Certain types of depression respond to tai chi. Many tai chi practitioners report a feeling of calm and oneness that emerges from tai chi postures and movements. These sensations bring a greater feeling of balance and provide relief from some of the symptoms of depression. A Massachusetts General Hospital study by Albert Yeung, MD, ScD, showed that Chinese Americans with mild to moderate depression who enrolled in a twelve-week tai chi class experienced a significant reduction in symptoms of depression as compared to control groups. Make a joint decision with your doctor about tai chi's value and how best to avail yourself of its therapeutic potential for you.

HELPS YOU CLEAR YOUR MIND

Quieting the mind supports all the tenets of tai chi. Our minds are capable of thinking (having thoughts) and of mindfulness (experiencing no thoughts). Tai chi teaches us to give up our thoughts and instead allow the balance between earth and heaven to lead us to mindfulness. Experiencing mindfulness means being fully present in the experience of the moment with clarity and inner peace. Our thoughts usually race into the past or the future. Mindfulness brings us into the present moment, relaxed and open. This state of emotional stillness seems outside of regular time and separate from the busy day. It is this state of stillness that will benefit you with full spirit and rejuvenation. Like a sitting meditation, the practice of tai chi creates a gate through which you can enter a world of stillness.

Learning to be open and ready to experience mindfulness can be a challenge at first. This oft-told story of an educated man coming before a master teacher might help you. "Hello," said the educated man, "my name is Professor Smith. I am a graduate of three universities and have authored books, articles, and research papers. I would very much like to learn from you."

"Won't you sit down?" invited the master.

"Thank you," the educated man replied as he sat upon a pillow near the teacher.

"Would you like some tea?" the master asked of him.

"Thank you, I would," the professor replied.

The master started pouring the tea into the professor's cup and continued pouring the tea until it spilled over the edges of his cup and into the saucer. Filling the saucer, he continued to pour as it spilled onto the table. Finally the astonished professor could hold back no longer. "My cup is full and the tea is spilling everywhere!"

The master looked at him, paused in his pouring, and said, "Yes, you come with a full cup. Your cup is already spilling over, so how can I give you anything? Come with emptiness, openness, or I can give you nothing."

Before a tai chi class or a practice, empty your cup. Release the events of the day. Let what you're holding on to drop away. Feel yourself begin to empty, to open and receive. Give up your preconceptions about what your practice time is going to bring you.

In Western culture, the body is usually doing one thing while the mind is doing another. Enormous amounts of stress build up as a result of these two different experiences going on at the same time. In the West, we have virtually no exercise or mental traditions that unite the two in a single, unified action. And yet the best way to reduce stress is to combine mind and body. Ten minutes of doing something where the body and mind are working together is more relaxing than two hours of activities that keep them separate.

Good body-mind activities include cooking, gardening, model car building, and so on. Each offers an opportunity to unify thought and action. Will the mind drift? Sure. But the action of the activity—cooking, gardening, model car building—calls the drifting mind back as incidents that require attention return.

The practice of tai chi expressly joins body and mind. As you learn tai chi and become more comfortable with the movements in practice, you will feel the same relaxation that occurs when your body and mind are absorbed in a good activity. But with tai chi, you will have the enormous added value of being involved in an ancient discipline that doesn't just stop with body-mind harmony. Recall that tai chi also fuels the chi, balances the yin and yang, and produces an array of health benefits.

To attain a state of mindfulness, do the following as best you can:

* Empty thoughts
* Empty expectations
* Empty performance
* Empty anxiety
* Empty comparison
* Empty competition

The irony is that to practice tai chi, an activity so full of gifts, you must come empty in order to know fullness.

TEACHES YOU TO SLOW DOWN

Your life is full. You rush from place to place and commitment to commitment, wishing for simplicity and a less hurried life. Everyone probably longs to have a life that is richer and happier, with meaningful work, well-adjusted kids, long-term friends, and a loving family and partner. These are needs that run across all humanity. But our built-up stress, our inability to rebound into a fresh and open emptiness each day, and the complexity of our lives have become enormous problems that stand in our way. Or perhaps we could say that we stand in our own way.

In order to achieve the level of contentment you want, you need effective tools for becoming truly resilient. Tai chi assists in this effort in the most helpful of ways. The lightness of the moves restores resiliency to joints and muscles, the deep breathing cultivates and nourishes the chi, and the disciplined style of motion balances the yin and yang within. Sleep becomes enough. Your sense of well-being strengthens. Your feeling of harmony and balance in the world is more apparent. Your patience with others is easy. No one is in your way. Your life is not unmanageable. Your stress melts into rest. The life fountain of pleasure, joyful simplicity, and rich meaning is yours to draw from because you're refilling it each day. Only an ancient form of movement could give so much.

The goal of a rewarding life is the same for everyone, even if the details differ. The reason these exercises have endured for thousands of years is because they deliver. They delivered then, and they deliver now. If anything, after having been honed by time, they deliver better now than ever before.

HARMONIZES YOUR MIND AND BODY

Tai chi students and teachers alike strive for the same symphony of body, mind, and breath. Stress occurs when the body is doing one thing and the mind is doing another—for example, the body is relaxing in a chair while the thoughts or feelings are engaged in a suspenseful book, movie, or TV show. The body takes on the thought and feeling of the mental experience. Your body, even though it is just sitting, feels the stress, anxiety, and concerns generated by the thoughts and feelings as you remain absorbed in the movie. This burdens your body with unrealized stress responses that include shortness of breath, an upset stomach, heart palpitations, and jumpiness. Even in sleep, the body will not completely discharge this stress. The next day you may bounce into the day, ready to go at it, and notice that your body seems tired. "Late night, probably," you might say, as you notice the symptoms of stress without considering the true cause. When the body and mind are not joined in a creative expressive interaction, the body takes the first hit in the form of reduced vitality and early aging. The mind takes a later hit when the sluggishness of the body finally slows it down too.

Everyday Meditation

A favorite meditation technique that requires nothing more than you and your life is to fully engage in whatever you are doing: washing dishes, walking, talking, silence, or anything else. It is this ability to engage in full presence with the simplest of activities that brings you more spiritual awareness of your true nature and disengages you from your more fearful habitual self. This full awareness in everyday activities sounds easy, but try it. Take some dishes and wash them for five minutes, staying completely focused on the task, even your breath, the whole time. It is very hard! It is a good endeavor because it shows how jumpy the mind is. It shows how hard it is to slow the jumpiness and how easy it is to drift from the present physical moment into a mental interlude.

This certainly doesn't mean you need to give up your relaxing pleasures. Instead, you can relax while cooking, engaging in a favorite sport, or designing or building something. Such activities are a bit more united as a single process and effort, with the body moving to support the requests of the mind. Even in these events, the mind may still jump to other subjects, maybe just for a nanosecond, but that's enough to break the union of body and mind.

Make no mistake, achieving a healthy harmony of mind and body is difficult. Our minds and feelings wander, and our bodies suffer. Most of your thoughts have nothing to do with the activity of the moment. They have to do with the past or the future. As a result, your ability to be in the moment isn't stable, because you are constantly being pushed and pulled by your bouncing mind. And because your feelings are directed by your thoughts, and because those thoughts are bouncing here and there, your feelings are not stable either. Your feelings then have little to do with whatever is happening at the moment.

Feelings are seldom a pure reaction to the moment. More often, they are influenced by thoughts that are going somewhere else. For example, suppose you've had a hard, long day and someone did something that got under your skin. You get home, and your kids are noisy. You tell them to quiet down. You shout. Your actions are the result of intrusive thoughts that, in turn, are driven by the irritated feelings you have about your coworker.

All this is unsettling for the body, of course. The body is deeply influenced by thoughts and feelings. Yet people seldom do anything that directly expresses thoughts or feelings through body action. As a result, their bodies are always stressed to some degree as they respond to all the bouncing thoughts and feelings. Unfortunately, this is the scattered state of the life that most everyone leads.

As you practice tai chi and make it part of your life, you can find a harmonious balance of mind and body. As you engage in the practice of mindfulness, you will begin to de-stress your body and help heal it. You'll see for yourself what happens. It will happen when you know tai chi well enough that it flows. It will happen when you're practicing in a place you enjoy. It will happen when you fully embrace the practice and your mind, movement, breath, and chi are all there, all moving in symphony with one another. Your thoughts will focus. Your feelings will stabilize, and you will be there, opening up to a world that you have yet to explore, a world of greater harmony, balance, and presence.

HARMONIZES YOUR BODY AND SOUL

Meditation provides a place in your inner life where your soul and your body can live in harmony. This is not an easy balance to achieve. The life of the body is completely concerned with survival, reproduction, and so forth. Contrast this to the life of your spirit. Filled with chi, your spirit wants to experience life and its changes. The spirit longs for wisdom as a result of growth generated by life and life's experiences. So you experience two very different agendas simultaneously, with the body saying, "I survive and play by my rules," and the spirit saying, "I experience and grow, and wisdom is mine." This tension between the body's need for security and the spirit's need to experience new challenges is a big problem. This tension can create personal confusion about how to achieve treasured goals. This tension can create illness, stress, early aging, and a lack of joy in ordinary existence. This struggle is core in human existence. It is true for everyone—rich or poor, healthy or not, people in all cultures and walks of life. It is this tension that moves through all ethnic and economic groups, creating a common ground for the powerful and powerless. It is life's great leveler.

The ancients had an ideal for finding balance between body and spirit. This ideal was sought by caring for the body's needs with a wise and supportive structure. In practical terms, this meant predictable meals, predictable sleep, no sudden changes, and letting the chi flow deeply into the body's tissues. Caring for the spirit was accomplished by trying to understand the true nature of one's self, to trust the great teachers, to uphold one's personal quality no matter what life brought, and to seek to elevate all of life by expressing personal standards. It was the union of these two "maintenance" programs that allowed the ancients to begin to see the wonder of a life lived with body and spirit balanced.

The ancients discovered that another world opened with a change of perspective, giving them refined wisdom on how to improve the quality of life for each person. This improvement then elevated the quality of standards for all. They saw that this work needed to be done inwardly by the individual. Their belief was that to change one's self in these ways would produce great, wise appreciation and love of life. It would also change others around this individual. Through this work, life would eventually evolve toward improvement.

Meditation was seen as the key to doing this inner work, and that these finer ways of being were impossible to achieve without it. This is the bottom line of Eastern philosophies. By practicing meditation, the tension between the body's need to survive and the spirit's need to grow in new ways finds balance, and so the tension between them diminishes. This harmony expresses itself in reduced body stress, a reduction of illness, and the slowing of the aging process.

CHAPTER 3

SPIRIT

Tai chi helps you feel your soul/spirit as a daily part of your life. You probably know people who race through their lives like chickens with their heads cut off. These people are so deeply involved with the details of life that they make no time for introspection and personal growth. As a result, they are unable to look deeply and gratefully at what has occurred and what is being learned. We also know wise people who seem to walk in a gracious, loving calm. Unflappable in stress, caring, concerned, and not pulled in a million different ways by life, they emanate a quiet courage and resiliency in their lives.

STRENGTHENS YOUR SPIRITUAL CONNECTION

The word *spiritual* in the dictionary has several slightly different definitions. The definition most relevant to tai chi is one that relates to conscious thoughts, emotions, and spirit. Tai chi attunes or adjusts you to your own conscious thoughts, emotions, and spirit.

Tai chi supports a personal faith, but it isn't a faith in itself. Even if you immerse yourself in the ideas of yin and yang and the *I Ching*, you're studying a philosophy, not a religion. So to do tai chi and attune yourself spiritually means to decide to do a practice that by its very nature returns you more deeply to yourself and to all the layers of self that you have. Your centering into your body and mind through these activities attunes you to you. Your self-awareness increases in all four areas—body, mind, emotion, and spirit.

This is not to say you will become self-absorbed. To be self-absorbed is to be unable to be present with anything or anyone. The world becomes a series of self-projections that serve only to process the introspection further. Self-awareness means that you know your own feelings and are so comfortable with them that you aren't ruled by your emotions. Instead, you appreciate them for their ability to connect you in empathy with the world around you. Your mind stays clear and unclouded by ruling your emotions; your mind leads you through one life event after another. You're calm, clear, unafraid, and yet deeply feeling—you are very human and connected.

Courage, resiliency, calm, wisdom, all of these come from one source—self-awareness: the knowledge of one's own nature. Self-awareness brings you the ability to take full responsibility for your actions so that you can view them with understanding. It fits people anywhere, anytime, in any faith. As tai chi practice deepens your awareness of yourself, and as your body and mind unite in clarity, your spirit within will also become clear.

HELPS YOU EMBRACE WU CHI, OR THE SOURCE OF ALL

Taoism is a faith that incorporates the concept of wu chi, an infinite nothingness. Everything in the universe is believed to evolve continually from this unknowable but accessible source. The purpose of life is to live in embodied balance, drawing from the source of wholeness, oneness, or nothingness. All actions of life are prisms through which we can experience the Tao's wholeness—be it in terms of health, medicine, communication, meditation, arts and music, business, and so on. Anything you can think of is a part of the Tao. Each movement of or into life is realized as a great potential for a personal experience of oneness. Each moment of life is permeated with a gift that embodies a deep sense of being connected to the wu chi, and that sense of connectedness can be embodied by anyone.

Balance is the key. The personal experience of health and well-being become ways for finding the wholeness—or the nothingness—or for letting it find you. You can express this balance through the practice of tai chi. Through tai chi you can engage this source, the wu chi, as a continual awareness in your daily life. Tai chi provides you with the perfect, nimble expression of balance that can illuminate your soul as it shines through the personality.

Every human behavior is a lens through which the wu chi flows into yin and yang (through tai chi). Tai chi in this sense isn't restricted to just the positions you learn in this book. Tai chi in this sense means that moment when stillness becomes movement. In this way a moving leaf and a gentle wind are also tai chi.

TEACHES YOU TO BALANCE YOUR CHI

Tai chi is where the wu chi divides into yin and yang. Everything in nature becomes a part of and is intertwined with these two forces of energy. Everything is included by yin (the feminine) and yang (the masculine), and they are included in everything. Yin and yang represent and express the natural harmonious polarity of all life.

Everything is subject to incline (or growth) and decline (or decay). Everything, even the smallest element, is growing one step at a time in an astonishing process of order and constant change. Your body, being an important part of nature, involves and expresses the properties of yin and yang. These are complementary polarities that divide at tai chi and then direct themselves to become unified in all forms of life. All phenomena, including everything that happens within your body, involve the interaction of these two energy forces.

Chi is spirited vitality (or energy) from the universe—wholeness or nothingness. Chi is the force within which the yin and yang flow. Your health and well-being depend upon how these flows move through your body. Yang flow is warm and active. Yin force is cool and receptive. You are affected by the amount of chi you've cultivated within and how the chi is circulating through the energy meridians of the body. The chi is cultivated and stored in the pelvic tan t'ien.

Tai chi also moves to create an inner environment for the proper balance of yin and yang. These flows are within the chi and move throughout the whole body, instilling the correct balance of the yin and yang energy force in each organ of the body as well as the meridian system. This meridian system circulates like little highways within the entire body. When the life force of chi is obstructed or when the balance of yin and yang within the organ is upset, illness occurs.

Tai chi supports the cultivation of chi and the continuing proper balance of yin and yang throughout the body. By doing tai chi on a regular basis, you can correct or avoid unwanted obstruction of the meridians (the chi highways throughout the body) and yin-yang imbalances.

Yin and yang, the balanced opposites, unite in tai chi. When yin and yang emerge to unite in tai chi, the level of balance or equality that occurs has to do with the nature of the intent that created the emerging flow. An angry mood or intent will carry more yang. A sad mood will carry more yin into the uniting. Tai chi is about restoring balance or equality within your daily life so you do not have excess yang or yin. By bringing your mind, body, and spirit into the place where these energies unite in harmony with the flows of yang and yin, you teach your mind, body, and spirit how to engage these flows in an equal unity. Your tai chi movement embodies the tai chi.

Tai chi is a movement meditation that balances and equalizes yin and yang as the uniting is happening within the body. This uniting within the body goes on ceaselessly. In fact, the Chinese belief is that the yin and the yang are always joining within you. You can't cease this uniting and also be alive, because the chi yin and yang is the very essence of life. It and you create your animation and liveliness according to your personal yin-yang balance, which, of course, changes constantly. This balance of yin and yang is shown next.

Yin and yang in balance

Suppose you lift weights, and you have bulk in your muscles. You're strong in these muscles, on the outside layers of your body. But let's also suppose you have had no inner training to match your outer strength. Further, you have had no instruction on how to develop your internal force. (This is the central theme in all martial arts—to cultivate, master, and direct your chi, which is your internal force.) You need more yin.

Too much yang

Now suppose you are timid. As a result, you have developed a life-style that is retreating. Your inner world is developed, but you are only truly comfortable in the privacy of your own home. You would be uniting yin and yang within you with an overabundance of yin. You need more yang—see the following image.

Too much yin

The Chinese believe that keeping the yin and yang in balance is the essence of youth, health, and well-being. The entire eternal cycle of life is designed to understand the two flows of essential chi, and to watch and record their tremendous influence.

Heaven and Earth in Balance As Well

Heaven is the yang chi, earth is the yin chi, and tan t'ien is where they join if the chi is properly directed. This is energetic balance.

So both a well-muscled (but poorly inner-developed) and inner-developed (but timid) person decide to take tai chi. The well-muscled person with too much yang learns about internal force—the quiet, receptive center within that's filled with personal stillness. A new sense of confidence enters this person. This individual will, perhaps, experience less conflict, have less need to maintain power over others, and enjoy an easier, more relaxed time with other people. The self-consciousness, as opposed to self-awareness, will diminish, and with it any inappropriate competitive, defensive, or demanding inclinations. This will all occur with no diminishment of power. Actually, the act of power, focus, and protection will become more effective. The yin and yang will again be in balance.

Ensure Good Health with Chi Balance

Balanced yin and yang energies are vital for good health—people become sick when this balance is broken. The circular movements of tai chi mirror this important balance. These physical activities also necessarily involve internal work, because mind and body participate in the same energies.

For the timid person with too much yin, the desire or need to retreat in order to feel confident and comfortable with oneself and life will begin to change. As yin and yang unite under the direction of the tai chi, new awareness will occur. A new inner confidence, one that emanates outwardly (yang) will grow and create a realization of inner confidence, but not just at home. It radiates outward, drawing a forward movement into life in a new way. Life seems more engaging, interesting, and not simply "too intense." Life is expanding, and more comfort and confidence is occurring. Released outer force has brought a needed and welcomed balance. The yin and yang energies now look more balanced.

EMPHASIZES POSITIVE ENERGY

Any person who has traveled to the East, particularly to China, has surely noticed groups of people of all ages doing tai chi together. (Now that tai chi is so well known throughout the world, this scene is everywhere—whether in a city park or on a cruise ship.) The Chinese consider themselves to be a very positive people, effective at achieving their goals, and tai chi is seen as an activity essential to this positive attitude.

As the chi is gathered and cultivated in the tan t'ien, it is then dispersed throughout the body. This chi differentiates into yin and yang flows through meridians. Twelve meridians run throughout the body like energy highways. Each meridian is associated with an organ. The name of the organ (lung, liver, and so on) refers to the physical organ and to the whole system of energy. Each organ has a unique energy flow, and it is this flow that runs in the meridians.

The meridians pass through the entire body: head, trunk, arms, and legs. All along these energy highways of specialized yin and yang are points that respond to stimulation. These are precise locations that are used to regulate the energy flow and, therefore, the functioning of the organ/meridian system. These meridians are regulated through acupuncture and acupressure, but even more so through tai chi practices.

Tai chi was developed to precisely harmonize these flows. Each step and hand movement is designed to put the meridian flows into accord with one another and with the larger universal system of energy flows. Each position has been given an element:

* A forward step: Metal
* A withdraw step: Wood
* Looking left: Water
* Looking right: Fire
* Central equilibrium: Earth

The movements are precisely designed to promote the correct energetic balance of the internal organs. It is no wonder so many people practice tai chi daily or why so many new learners are jumping on board each day!

OFFERS A CONNECTION TO NATURE

Yin and yang and the balance you achieve with them has great effect on every aspect of your being. Emotional, physical, mental, and spiritual health are all guided by them. In keeping with this concept, Chinese medicine observes five elements: water, fire, wood, metal, and earth. The elements, because they spring from nature, may seem separate from us. But they are considered to be a dynamic process that is essential for understanding the movements of and through nature, people included. These elements are seen as dynamic, interactive, and that from which all life is made. Each element carries its own unique qualities:

* Water: Soaks and moves downward
* Fire: Heats and moves upward
* Wood: Can be shaped into curved or straight pieces
* Metal: Can be melted, molded, and hardened
* Earth: Provides a place for seeds to grow

When these five elements interact, each one is changed by the interaction. Those interactions show us several cycles: mutual creation, mutual closeness, mutual destruction, and mutual fear.

Mutual Creation
One element produces another in an endless cycle of creation:

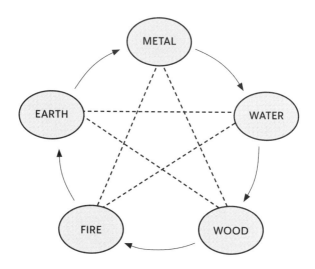

The cycle of creation

* Wood creates fire: Two sticks together can create fire.
* Fire creates earth: Fire creates ash, which is absorbed into the earth.
* Earth creates metal: Metal is found in the earth.
* Metal creates water: When metal is heated and cooled, condensed water forms, and at high temperatures, metal melts into liquid.
* Water creates wood: Water helps grow trees that become wood.

Mutual Closeness

Wood is close to water. Water is close to metal. Metal is close to earth. Earth is close to fire. Fire is close to wood.

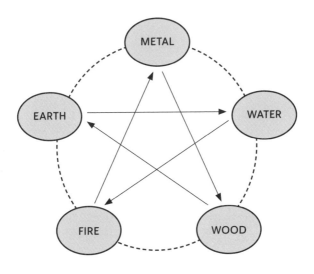

Mutual closeness

Mutual Destruction

This principle presents conflicts between elements:

* Wood weakens earth: Wood leaches elements from earth.
* Earth limits water: Earth contains water's movement, as in lakes and dams.
* Water puts out fire.
* Fire weakens metal: Fire weakens metal's great strength by melting it.
* Metal destroys wood by cutting it.

Mutual Fear

Because of mutual destruction, each element has a respect for or a fear of the element that can weaken it. For example, fire fears water, because water extinguishes fire.

People Share Traits with the Five Elements

People are also seen to be made up of the five elements. The composition or interaction of these elements makes up the nature of the person, gives clues to self-understanding and knowing other people, and provides vital information about the best route to health.

The elements and how they affect us is complex, but a very simple summary is as follows:

* Wood: An active, direct person
* Metal: A contained person
* Fire: An intense, quick-to-respond person
* Water: An emotional person
* Earth: A solid, nurturing person

Traditional Chinese medicine incorporates these natural elements into its approach to healing. These principles of the five elements and their guidelines are applied to physiology, pathology, diagnosis, and therapy. In diagnosing or understanding the imbalances that are believed to contribute to disease, the organs of the body are divided into yin (solid organs) and yang (hollow organs). Each organ has a corresponding element:

* Heart: Fire
* Spleen: Earth
* Lungs: Metal
* Kidney: Water
* Liver: Wood
* Small intestine: Fire
* Stomach: Earth
* Large intestine: Metal
* Bladder: Water
* Gall bladder: Wood

This theory of the five elements and their relationship to one another throughout all of life—people and events—has been used in Chinese medicine to maintain health and cure illness. So deeply did these ancient doctors believe in their ability to create health using this model that they are said to have accepted payment only when they were able to keep the patient well. If the patient became diseased, the doctor took no payment until health or balance had returned. If this lore is true, it highlights the mutual partnership of the doctor-patient relationship. The patient was a regular, committed, and conscientious participant in his or her own wellness by following the guidelines that the doctor laid out, and the doctor accepted full responsibility if the outlined program did not work. This type of equal and mutual partnership in the maintenance of health is wonderful to consider.

Tai chi, of course, is fundamental in this approach to being in harmony with the eternal cycle of life. Your capacity is directly related to the amount of chi you have circulating within.

Mixing Your Practice with Observations from Nature

The great tai chi masters did not have TV, smartphones, or computers. They could not turn to the Internet for inspirational videos. Instead, they experienced life by being very much a part of nature. From their observations, they applied their interpretations. For this reason, many positions in tai chi are described with a metaphor from the natural world. Crouching Tiger, White Crane Spreads Its Wings, and High Pat on Horse are just three of many tai chi poses that are inspired by nature. If you're having a bit of a problem really getting one of the postures, take a walk. Venture into nature, stroll down the street, step into a park, hike up a hillside, gaze at the sky, or watch animals on leashes or at the zoo. Use whatever is available in nature.

Seeing medical treatment as an interrelationship rather than a singular fix (which is usually the case in Western medicine, where, for example, we treat one organ for an illness), practitioners of Chinese medicine treat the whole body. They study the relationships between organs and systems and approach treatment based on those interactions. The belief is that bringing balance to the dysfunctional organ restores balance in the entire body. This intricate system of rebalancing is usually not achieved simply by taking some medicine. Instead, the solution is to approach the imbalance from a whole perspective.

The five elements and how they apply to everything is understood through the various relationships that can exist—creative, close, destructive, fearful. Once the element-interaction source of the health problem is uncovered, various tools are applied to create a balance:

* Acupuncture and acupressure points are stimulated along the meridians (chi highways throughout the body) to level chi flow.
* Herbal remedies are given to bolster the body's reserves and give nourishment where needed.
* Breathing instructions are given.
* Tai chi is recommended for exercise.

Arts, music, silence, and meditation are all part of a program of lifelong health. Everything in life that you are affected by is analyzed from the perspective of your attitude toward the event and whether your attitude balances or unbalances you.

IMPROVES YOUR RESILIENCY

Resilience is a wonderful word. It means the ability to return to an original form after being bent, compressed, or stretched; the ability to recover from an illness, depression, adversity, or the like; and the ability to spring back or rebound.

When you've a bad day, a traumatic life challenge, or just a busy life, the stress of it shows in the tense muscles in your shoulders, legs, wrists, back, ankles, and so on. It would be great if we could regain this natural elasticity with deep sleep alone, but this is not enough. As children, we rebalance in sleep for twelve to thirteen hours. As adults, however, all too often we get six or fewer hours of sleep.

This lack of sleep is from our lives being so full. By the time you do everything you're committed to, it is late at night, and to continue the commitments, you have to rise early. This says nothing of interrupted sleep from car alarms, sick babies, anxious thoughts, indigestion, poor health, low estrogen—the list is endless! The few hours of sleep you do get just isn't enough for your body to completely unwind, for your unconscious mind to work out the day through dreams, and for you to achieve the rebalancing of the body, mind, and spirit.

With the diminishment of deep and restful sleep comes a diminishment of resilience. The days hit you harder. You get less pleasure from your activities. You run, work out, and do yoga, but that deep lack of resilience continues to build. Your need for resilience may be one of the most important reasons for practicing tai chi. Tai chi emphasizes softness and flexibility, lightness and agility in movement, and helps return resilience to your body, mind, and spirit.

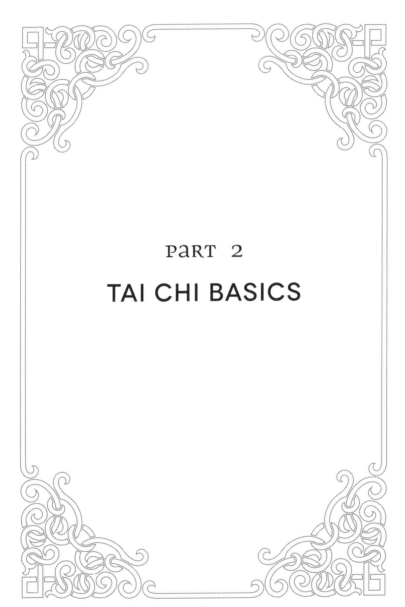

PART 2

TAI CHI BASICS

CHAPTER 4

PREPARING YOURSELF TO PRACTICE

Before starting your tai chi practice, you can make some preparations to ensure that it will be more enjoyable and easier to stick to. By developing great habits, such as creating a pleasant space for these activities, inviting a friend to practice with you, playing beautiful music, and wearing comfortable clothing, your tai chi practice will be a joy in your daily life.

CREATING A SPACE

No matter how large or small your home, try to dedicate a space for your tai chi practices so that when you enter this area your body knows it's tai chi time. The following sections can help you set up this area (which may also be your living room when you're not practicing tai chi!).

The Size of Your Space

To accomplish tai chi successfully, you only need a few square feet of open area. Because you can also take tai chi with you wherever you go, you can do it on a lovely beach, in the park with friends, or on a mountaintop with a great view.

Safety

You want a space to move in that is safe—no pets or small children racing through, no smooth or slippery surfaces. You want a large enough space so you can stretch out your arms and rotate without rapping your knuckles on something. Don't practice tai chi near the tops of stairs, edges of buildings, curbs, or on any uneven surface. You want a space that's secure underfoot where there is enough space to move safely without anything to knock over or bump into.

Air Quality

Fresh air is, of course, best. Just do your best if the air where you live is not always clear. At the same time, there is no point in doing breath exercises if you're filling your lungs with toxins. If you live in a smoggy area, practice when the air is the clearest—this may be morning or later evening. Or find a spot in front of your air purifier or air conditioner (both of these help clear the air). If you're in a really polluted area, get a mask to filter out many of the pollutants. If you do have clear air, open the windows and doors or go outside.

Lighting

In China, there is a big emphasis on practicing tai chi in natural light. The idea is that the light carries chi, or life energy, and so you want to exercise in an environment where the chi is plentiful. Sunlight in the very early morning is a revered time for energy-enhancing movement. Do you have a yard available or space in a room that has an abundance of natural light? If so, practice tai chi there if you can. Open windows allow the light and fresh air to fill your tai chi space. Even if your light is artificial or limited, you can still practice tai chi.

Audiovisual Equipment

Though you should limit screens as part of your tai chi practice, at first it might help to follow along with a video that shows you the postures and poses. If so, be sure you can easily see your TV, tablet, laptop, or smartphone.

Adding Sound

If you find music or nature sounds a valuable backdrop for your practice, feel free to add them! Natural sounds such as waves on a beach, birdcalls, and wind blowing through trees are very relaxing. Sequoia Records has a nice selection of relaxing music. Check out their collection online at www.sequoiarecords.com.

FINDING PROPER CLOTHING

In tai chi you'll be rotating and moving your arms and legs, and your belly will be moving in and out with a free-flowing breath. This is not the time for snug-fitting clothes or for clothes made of heavy fabric. This is the time for a relaxed, comfortable fit, and an easy-to-wear outfit made from a lighter-weight fabric. Stay away from denim, but T-shirts are fine. Do you have a favorite outfit for your downtime? This may be a perfect tai chi outfit—one that's especially comfy, especially relaxing. Any clothing you wear in your practice should be comfy, light, and flexible so you can move and breathe.

The shoes you choose are also important. Traditional tai chi shoes look more like slippers than shoes. It is for a good reason. First and foremost, you don't want to slip, and so tai chi slippers have nonslip soles. Second, you don't want to catch one foot on the other while moving. For this reason, tai chi slippers fit well, but not tightly, and are flexible. You also want your shoes to be lightweight. Tai chi slippers are made of cloth, and they are often basic in color—black, white, or navy blue. Tai chi slippers are easy to find online.

If you choose not to get tai chi slippers, use a nonslip, lightweight, flexible shoe for your practice. Without good support, the balance and confidence that come from the practice will be compromised, so be sure your footwear is suitable for these specific exercises.

READYING YOUR MIND

As you get ready for your tai chi practice, recognize that you will be entering an ancient movement, a movement that carries its own color-ful, rich history that has evolved into an exercise that promotes better health. Be receptive and committed.

Harmonize Your Body and Mind

Much of what you will be learning in tai chi surpasses just memo-rizing positions. You are working toward a union of your body and mind. Your mind directs your body in consistent, sequenced, and graceful motions and, in so doing, is constantly drawn back from its restless wanderings. Because your mind is completely present in each moment, this practice of tai chi allows you to engage in a type and level of attention that leads to heightened awareness.

This habit of blended concentration can be used in all areas of your life. Usually in our culture the body is doing one thing (driving, running, sitting, or eating) and the mind is doing something entirely different (thinking about work, watching traffic, enjoying a concert, or carrying on a conversation). You can't truly appreciate the value of the body and mind in coordinated union until you've experienced it. You can practice a bit before beginning the exercises by being mindful of, say, walking to your tai chi space. How much of your body do you feel? Feel your legs as they propel you forward, your feet as they roll from heel to toe on the surface. Notice your breath. Think about your tan t'ien deep in the pelvis. Tai chi perfects this body-mind union, and the consequential growth in concentration, focus, attention, and relaxation you gain is amazing.

Remember Circular Breathing Methods

Tai chi emphasizes circular breathing. Imagine you're breathing in a continuous breathing pattern. Remember the tan t'ien, the energy center storage spot for chi and the spot from which each breath circles. An inhaled breath is drawn down by the tan t'ien and goes further down into the perineum. As the inhale continues, the breath travels up the spine, into the head, and out the nose. On the exhale, the breath is exhaled out, and the golden chi floats through the front of the body. Of course, it goes into your lungs as well!

This is the difference between breath and chi: your breath goes into your nose and lungs to send oxygen throughout your body. The chi also goes into the nose and lungs, but being very light and permeable energy, it isn't confined to the avenues of the breath. It has its own avenues throughout the body—the meridians (chi highways throughout the body). The chi can also be directed by the mind. As you breathe in and out and your nose and lungs do their job of providing oxygen to the body, chi also flows into the body as you inhale, then circulates, and then exhales as you exhale. Chi travels on its own avenues and can be directed with intent.

Take Tai Chi with You

Because you can take tai chi with you, it's a very flexible exercise program. People who travel for a living need to exercise. With some areas of cities not safe to run in and with gyms sometimes hard to find, it is great to have tai chi available on those overnight trips.

As you practice tai chi, imagine your breath (chi) running anywhere: down your arm, through your head, out your feet, moving from you to another person. It is all chi, but the breath is a terrific way to allow it to be more real. As you work with circular breathing, you'll find that the movement of the breath/chi helps you lift your arms, lengthen your back, and soften your knees. Your breath/chi will become at one with the movements as you use your mind to direct the breath/chi. So in circular breath, your mind and body are functioning together.

Turn Off Your Phone

Is your smartphone set to Do Not Disturb mode? This is your time to tune out the outer world and tune in to the rebalancing experience of being in your inner world. Silence your phone and take a short break from your outer world. Embrace your opportunity to be in your breath, in your movement, and in your body-mind unification.

Imagine an Invisible Practice Screen

This screen is around and surrounding your practice place. Like a window screen, it is fine enough mesh that nothing gets through that you don't want in your space. When you walk through this screen, it filters or screens out all your stress, pressures, and unfinished or yet-to-be-accomplished business of the day. It filters out all feelings and thoughts that interfere with the quiet, centered pleasure of your practice. Then when you're finished, you can pick them up again as you walk out. Or just pick up the ones you want and let the others melt away.

Imagine You're Embarking on a Mini Vacation

Do you have a spot on earth that you love? Bring your five senses there. Smell it, hear it, see it, touch it, taste it. Let your body feel what it would be like to be there. When you're ready, start your practice.

Be Thankful

After you enter wherever your practice space is, say a word of quiet thanks to all those who have gone before you in tai chi. Recognize before you start that you're now engaging in an ancient, loved art.

READYING YOUR BODY

Just as you prepared your space and your mind, you should be sure your physical body is ready to begin tai chi as well. Here are some ways to accomplish that.

Practice at Your Low Time of the Day or Night

Most everyone has a time of day when their energy is lower than at other times. Early to midafternoon is a common time to feel flat. Other people feel that way first thing in the morning. For them, a slow start on the day is essential. Still others find dusk a perfect relaxation time.

Are you an insomniac? Tai chi at three in the morning can be a great time filler when you can't sleep, plus it can rebalance you energetically and make the night less unpleasantly wakeful.

Practice When Your Stomach Is Empty

It takes a lot of energy to digest food. Some people get tired after a meal and are less mentally clear, even groggy. That is a time for a walk, a quiet moment, a quick siesta, but not a great time for a practice. When your stomach is a little light, you may be a bit tired but not groggy, so this is a great time for tai chi.

Drink a Cup of Green Tea

Green tea has a bit of caffeine. It opens the breath (and also reduces gum disease). The masters used it in the morning before meditation to help stay awake.

Get Rid of Aggression

If you've come to your practice feeling aggressive or competitive and you can't get into the flowing motions, take a break. Do something strenuous—run, hit a punching bag, lift weights—and then begin your tai chi session.

Use Foot Lotion

Rub some special foot lotion on your feet. Just make sure it is all rubbed in before you start your practice so you don't slip!

Relax Your Ankles and Wrists

It can be very helpful to open the "gates" of the ankles and wrists just prior to practice. One at a time, rotate your feet and stretch your toes. Put your pointer finger between the tendons of your big and second toe. Run your finger slowly up your foot until you find the indentation just before the rise on the top of your foot. Rub this point on each foot for a while—it opens the upward flow of chi in the body. Now rotate your hands, stretch your fingers, and bend your hands forward and back just a bit. Shake your hands. Close your thumbs against your palms.

Remove Jewelry
This is especially true if they circle your neck, waist, fingers, ankles, or wrists. Jewelry can alter energy flows.

Relax Your Belly
Breathe while thinking of your tan t'ien (see Chapter 1). Now you can relax. No need to hold your tummy in. Just relax into your belly. Let the breath drop more and more deeply into your center. Relax into your tan t'ien and feel the fullness of the chi begin to accumulate.

Develop a Pre-Practice Ritual
Develop a familiar ritual to do just prior to your practice, such as drinking a cup of your favorite beverage or taking a few quiet moments to rest and relax your tensions. Sit quietly in a chair, enjoy a view, splash some cool water on your face, breathe a fragrance...you'll think of more ideas. Any activity like this creates a ritual space.

CONSIDERING A CLASS OR TEACHER

If you're a beginner, taking a class is a great way to start your tai chi practice. It can also help you stay accountable for going: if you've paid in advance, you will be far less inclined to dodge a class, or if you must miss one, you'll probably be more inclined to take a make-up class.

Choosing a Class Format

Tai chi is a solo exercise. It can be done with a group, but it doesn't rely on group interaction. It is always better, then, to be involved in a type of instruction that gives quality personal attention. Classes are usually about forty-five minutes to an hour long. Following are some options:

* Private instruction, if you can afford it and find an instructor who teaches this way, is best.
* Another option is a small class. You could get a few friends together, find a good instructor and a good location, and relax with some tai chi.
* If you're in a regular-sized class, make sure you get attention focused just on you. Ask questions and seek clear teaching. If your teacher seems to dislike this attempt for extra attention, the class may be too big to manage extra attention graciously. See whether the teacher has a smaller class or initiate a conversation on ways to solve the problem.
* If there are no classes near you, try learning from a video of a master or a reputable *YouTube* source.

A good class should offer the following:

* A pleasing, well-lit space that allows plenty of space for free movement.
* A time of silence at the beginning.
* A brief but effective warm-up.
* A demonstrated review of what has been learned to date.

* The name and explanation of new positions.
* A clear demonstration of new positions with new steps taught in a uniform manner.
* Modification due to special needs made with gracious understanding.
* A breakdown of new steps into manageable pieces.
* Repetition of new steps.

You probably won't hear a lot of talking—verbal instruction is usually minimal. The instructor will probably give you the name of the position in a quiet way that matches the gentle movements.

If you're in a large room, you should be able to see the instructor or class helpers easily. Each teaching person should be positioned in a way that right, left, north, south, east, and west are clear and don't require the student to change his or her position to see various aspects of the movement. This extra movement is guaranteed to add to the confusion, as it interferes with muscle memory.

How to Find a Great Teacher

You can find many varieties of tai chi classes and instructors. This leaves the choice of a teacher, the form, the level of ancient influence, and the style of learning all very much up to you. Following are some qualities to look for in an instructor.

Relaxation

Your teacher should be relaxed and calm from head to toe. It will look as if every part of his or her body is at ease. Because each movement is led by an engaged mind, the movements flow in a remarkable way. Done properly, your instructor's movements will be smooth and have a soothing effect on the observer as well as the practitioner. You want a practitioner who does the movement out of a personal love for it and a teacher who moves in an even, slow manner—a manner that demonstrates the details of movement in a way that they are clear for your learning.

Constant Improvement

Look for a teacher who is constantly working to upgrade his or her personal degree of success in coordinating physically, mentally, and emotionally within the practice of the movements.

Search for a teacher who has clear savvy of the continuous and circular movements. The shoulders will be relaxed and dropped, while his or her arms will hang in a relaxed manner from the shoulder joints. The elbows will point down and are never leading the movements. The balance will look as if the body weight balances on a straight line, with the root firmly positioned in only one foot at a time.

Discipline

Another key ingredient to good teaching (and good learning) is commitment and personal discipline. A teacher who understands discipline as a tool to create experiences that improve life is perfect. This is opposed to a teacher who loves discipline simply for its own sake. The first will provide teaching that allows you to become your own best teacher. The second will never let you go beyond the teacher's need to control your learning.

A good teacher will place a gentle, firm emphasis on breathing. The teacher will encourage the breathing to be natural, ever-deepening, slow, and matching the movement with both synchronized and blended skill. No tai chi movement can begin to fulfill itself without proper skill.

Knowledge of Tai Chi Philosophy

Look for a teacher who has a good understanding of the knowledge and philosophy of tai chi. This can add extra pleasure to your learning. I also like a teacher who understands that tai chi and other similar practices are undergoing a great transition as they spread across the world, so that no one way can be considered the best method or even a standard method. When anything goes through expansion, experimentation, or exchange of opinions, an open forum of sharing and valuing is essential for this change. Tai chi is always changing, and new standards will evolve over time.

Always Observe a Class

In order to determine whether a teacher demonstrates these qualities, you will need to observe the class. This is a reasonable request, and you should not be charged a fee for viewing.

There should, however, be no argument on the most basic, fundamental aspects of tai chi, for these remain constant. Your teacher should have a good grasp of them, love teaching them, and recognize that variations on this theme are occurring everywhere.

Join a Friend

If you can't take a class but want to commit to a particular time to practice, consider finding a friend to meet with at appointed times. Even if you're both tired and want to give up the class, you'll be more likely to practice if you have to meet your friend. Two or more people create interesting opportunities for sharing and story swapping, and you can all witness the positive changes in each other as a result of your commitment to your practice.

Getting Individualized Attention

In ancient times tai chi was taught on a one-to-one basis: one teacher to one student. These days you're more likely to find small group sessions. If you're in a class and feel that you're not getting enough quality attention, speak to the teacher. See if you can work out some individual time before or after class. Often a bit of one-to-one is a nice support for a class environment.

ADOPTING A LEARNER'S ATTITUDE

In ancient China, learning tai chi required satisfying vigorous standards that demonstrated one's abilities to respond to the demands of the discipline. Students didn't have the option of practicing the postures when they were in the mood or had the time. Instead, tai chi was a way of life. They were a work of commitment and carried all the expectations for performance and success that commitment to your career may have for you.

The Ancient Ways

The instructor was a revered mentor/master who hand-selected one or two students and endeavored to pass on his considerable wisdom to them. The structure of the teaching was rigid. This disciplined style of teaching and learning nurtured a deep and trusting relationship between the master and student. The master, like most people when they grow older, wanted to pass along the wisdom he had accumulated over decades of experience and learning. The student wanted to improve himself by meeting challenges, mastering them, and leaving his mark on the world.

To be chosen by a master teacher was desired by all students of the martial arts. It was only in gaining the master's interest that one could improve his skills. The teachings were secret and highly protected. For a talented student who lacked a bit of something and was therefore not chosen, the future had a firm limit, a wall that he would never pass through.

For the chosen student, on the other hand, the sky was the limit. Now available to him was all the accumulated wisdom of a master's lineage, which he could begin to embody.

China was a culture in which one's life path was controlled by the class into which one was born. Options were further controlled by gender. (To get into the martial arts schools and temples you had to be a man.) One way to move beyond the usual class restrictions was to be accepted by a master if you had exceptional martial arts talent. You can imagine how intense the competition was. For every man chosen, thousands remained in the wings.

Martial Arts Titles

The following are titles of mastery in martial arts:

- Sien-sun: Firstborn, someone who knows more than you because he was born before you
- Lao-sze: Old teacher, a wise and venerated person of any age
- Chiao-sou: College professor
- Si-fu: Expert, teacher, father—children who apprenticed and became a part of the teacher's life

With all the cultural pressure and personal desire to excel, the student who was finally accepted approached this teaching as a privilege that had been bestowed—a golden opportunity. His goal became to gather enough skill that he, too, could be a master in the lineage, a credit to his master and his school, and a master of martial arts in his own right. Perhaps if he studied hard, practiced with great discipline, competed with others and won continuously, meditated, and had great spiritual growth, he would become a great master known throughout the country and remembered beyond his time. He could be a man whom others looked to over the centuries because of the great balance he had developed between martial art and gentle spiritual wisdom.

This excitement, clarity of purpose, and discipline was what was behind the student who entered his first training session. Of course he entered in reverence, honoring both the teacher and the discipline that could make such a great desirable difference in his life. This master longed to pass along his wisdom and continue the lineage. This was a personal but also a cultural goal, and it created a need to be a mentor beyond what most people experience today. They both came together, filled with hope for the outcome. They honored each other for the excellence each expressed. They respected each other and the tradition that drew them together. All this happened before the first instruction.

A Modern Interpretation

If you want to be a committed student of tai chi, you should respect the art itself and be focused on your spiritual growth. As you embody the movements that have been passed down all these centuries, the same gift is there, the same capacity to become filled with inner peace and be in great physical shape. Tai chi will open up more each day. In this gentle unfolding lies the treasures that have made this skill so valued. If you want to know these gifts, commit to take the time each day to practice and learn.

TROUBLESHOOTING COMMON ISSUES

Three areas frequently interfere with being able to benefit from tai chi, but don't worry too much about them. Let the sequences come in their own time, at their own pace. Do keep the following information in mind, but don't stress about it.

Figuring Out How to Keep Your Entire Body Moving

Every movement involves the entire working body. It can sometimes be easy to forget to move both hands simultaneously and, if you're standing, to move both legs simultaneously as well.

Learning to Have Solid and Empty Limbs

As you practice tai chi, you will learn about the concept of "solid and empty" for your legs and arms. You are probably unaccustomed to thinking of or feeling your arms and legs this way. You can do a little preview practice by shifting the weight to one leg and letting that leg become solid. The other leg, with less weight on it, meanwhile is hollow. You can do the same with your arms. Push with one as the other rests. The one you're pushing with is solid. The arm at rest is hollow.

Cultivating a Body-Mind Balance

Uniting your body and mind can be tricky at first. We have created a culture in which many of us don't do physical work. Instead, our work is mostly mental, and the body is not well used. Even for those who do physical work, the mind is often elsewhere. Whether yours is a life of a poorly used body and an active mind or a well-used body and a traveling mind, from a tai chi perspective, the basic problem is the same: the body and the mind are not unified. Even if you bike, run, or walk, your mind is still traveling. It is only in the most arduous athletics—the Tour de France, a long triathlon, or perhaps a marathon—that the mind binds with the body in a common expression. Most people, however, don't have this type of physical endurance as a regular part of their lives. Instead, life is a continual, continuous example of mind and body on two separate agendas. It is obvious the body gets the short end of the stick if you are sedentary, but actually both the mind and the body are cheated. When the mind and body are in the same experience, united in the same effort, there is a focus, a centeredness, an absorption in the task at hand that quiets both the mind and body. It is as if these two sides of ourselves can do things apart, but like any good partnership, they are much better together.

When Should You Practice?

Do your practice at the most convenient time possible. The Chinese masters probably did it at the first morning dew, but you may need to make time for a long drive to work or be available to help get the kids ready for their day. So perhaps morning isn't for you. You may have some time just before you drop into bed at night. Let your practice time be simple—not a big deal—just a period when you gather yourself in before you say goodbye to the day. Slide it in where it works.

This cultivation of the body and mind acting in unison is fundamental to tai chi. This may be the single most important gift tai chi imparts. When the mind and body act as one, the soul, spirit, or inner depth within is at peace. Having the body and mind as one reduces mental stress and that, in turn, improves focus. The body-mind balance keeps your mind from drifting into negativity. (The mind is too busy trying to figure out tricky little tai chi positions!) The body is enhanced by the presence of the mind, for then it becomes more alive and in tune with the world around it. Tai chi gives the mind an opportunity to guide the body, and it gives the body the ability to be more engaged and in tune with the mind's love of learning. The sum total is a deep quieting within. A sense of rightness in the order of things becomes more accessible. You feel in yourself and with yourself—calm, centered, present, and alert.

BASIC TAI CHI PRINCIPLES

Before you begin doing postures and poses, it's a good idea to understand the core concepts behind this ancient movement art. Keep these in mind as you practice the movements in the next chapters. Following are basic principles of tai chi.

Relaxation
Take a few minutes to release a bit of the tightness in the muscles. Put your fingers to your forehead, lightly touching the skin, and let the thoughts that fill your frontal lobe just drift away.

Emptiness and Fullness
Be ready to let your body partake of the experience of emptiness and fullness that is tai chi.

Evenness and Slowness
Prepare for even and slow postures. Allow a grace of movement to occur as you evenly and slowly move from one posture to the next.

Balance
As the spine is straight and vertical, practice shifting weight in your legs. This shifting of weight creates easier grace and allows a steady balance.

Rooting and Sinking

The outcome of relaxing and sinking into the positions is to root the feet, as if roots have sprung from your feet and penetrate deep into the earth. When you are rooted from the pelvis, legs, and feet, it is very difficult to become unbalanced mentally, emotionally, or physically.

Coordination and Centering

As you keep your attention on the tan t'ien, you ensure that all movements flow from there as a complete unit. The body coordinates with the mind, the mind coordinates with the breath, the breath coordinates with the body, and so the circle goes.

Breathing and Chi

Generally one inhales breath/chi whenever the arms are pulled backward or contracted, and the exhale occurs when the arms are stretched, raised, or pushed forward. This breathing is done with the focus on the tan t'ien, and with the breath sitting in the tan t'ien.

Meditation

Unlike other forms of meditation you may already be familiar with, tai chi is a standing meditation—stances one takes to quiet the mind, relax the body, and promote the accumulation of chi.

CHAPTER 5

WARM UP

Any good exercise program should begin with a warm-up. The purpose of warming up is to literally heat the muscles and joints and increase the circulation of blood. Warming up on a daily basis will improve your flexibility and balance over time, and it will also reduce the amount of tension that builds up in your body.

Cross Crawl

You start this warm-up by walking in place and touching your left knee with your right hand and then alternating, touching your right knee with your left hand. Start quite slowly, and if you want, you can speed up to running in place. Do this for thirty to ninety seconds.

Cross Crawl

Cross Crawl with Twist

Continuing to walk, increase the twist in the movement by reaching past your knee and twisting your spine. If desired, look in the direction of your twist to bring the twist into the neck as well. As the left knee rises, twist across it to the left side and so forth. Do this at an easy pace for thirty to ninety seconds.

Cross Crawl with Twist

Infinity Arms

Continuing to walk in place, swing your arms to trace a horizontal figure eight or infinity sign in front of you. You can clasp the hands or just keep the palms relatively close to each other. Start drawing the X of the infinity sign going down.

Infinity Arms 1

As one knee rises, the hands go down across it, and then rise and go down across the next knee as it rises. Do this for about thirty seconds, and then switch directions. When you switch directions, draw the X going up across the rising knee. Do this for thirty seconds.

Infinity Arms 2

Shoulder Rolls

Roll your shoulders, alternating circling each so that as one shoulder goes up, the other goes down. Do this about seven times, and then reverse the direction. Roll that side about seven times. When you're done, shake out your arms.

Shoulder Rolls

Hula Pelvis

Standing with your feet hip-width apart, put your hands on your hips and rotate your hips in large circles five or six times each direction. The weight should circle in your feet as you do this.

Hula Pelvis

Sexy Pelvis

Let your arms hang and roll your pelvis as you keep your weight mostly central. Move slowly and try to make this movement smooth. Do this about seven times in each direction.

Foot Figure Eight

This is a range-of-motion exercise for the hip joints and is also an excellent balance drill. If your balance is precarious, stand near something so that you can catch yourself. You may want to keep one hand on the back of a chair or on a wall. If you do, try to use the wall or chair only as reassurance and keep your contact with it very light.

Foot Figure Eight 1

Standing on one leg with that knee a bit bent, use your lifted foot to draw a figure eight on the floor. Locate the middle of the figure directly beneath your hip so that there is a circle in front of you and a circle behind you. After seven repetitions, draw the figure eight in the other direction. Repeat this on the other side. Make the figure eights nice and full and rounded. Notice how different the movement in the hip is from one direction to the next.

Foot Figure Eight 2

Wrist Swirls

Although this is a range-of-motion drill for the wrist, you can also use it as a balance drill by lifting one foot off the floor. Make sure to slightly bend the knee of the standing leg. Extend the arm opposite of the lifted leg in front of your body and swirl the wrist first one direction and then the other, about five times. Do this at a leisurely pace. If your flexibility is good, bring your foot up behind you and hold it there. This will give you a nice stretch as well. Repeat on the other side.

Wrist Swirls

Ankle Swirls

You can use this range-of-motion exercise for the ankle as a balance drill. Stand on one leg with the knee bent and lift the other foot off the ground. Swirl the ankle seven times in one direction and seven times in the other. Do this at a leisurely pace and make the swirls as smooth as you can. If your flexibility it good, bring the knee of the swirling leg up and clasp it to the chest with both arms, getting a nice stretch.

Ankle Swirls

Elbow Massage

This exercise works best with naked elbows. Start with your left palm on the front of your right elbow with your right palm near the left hip.

Elbow Massage 1

Slide your palm around the elbow, following the fingertips over the point of the elbow. Bring the right arm up inside the left while the elbow rotates on the left palm until the right forearm points away from the body.

Elbow Massage 2

Bring your left hand up the inside of the elbow and over the crease while the right palm goes back to the left hip. The movement should be smooth with both arms always moving. Keep the pressure between your hand and elbow firm, warm, and loving.

Do this seven times and then reverse. (In the reverse direction, your right arm goes down inside the left. After seven times on this side, repeat both directions.)

Plié

Tai chi borrows the plié from ballet as a wonderful warm-up for the legs and groin muscles. This is the ballet exercise in which the dancer bends and straightens the knees while standing in place.

Stand with your feet turned out from each other. The exact distance between the heels and the angle of your feet is determined by how low down you go and how flexible you are in the groin. For heel spacing, when you're at your lowest, the line of your lower leg should be vertical.

Plié 1

For the foot angle, keep the thigh in the same line as the foot. If you can open the groin more throughout the rise and fall of the exercise, turn your feet out a bit more to accommodate your flexibility. Don't strain. After you've established the shape of your stance, bend your knees until your thighs are no lower than horizontal. Then straighten the knees, but don't lock them and don't change the angle of your thighs at the groin.

Plié 2

If you like, you can raise your arms as you go down and lower them as you go up. Remember to keep your body upright. It can be helpful to imagine that you're keeping your tailbone, shoulders, and the back of your head flat on a wall as you go up and down. Repeat the movement about ten times.

CHAPTER 6

STRETCHING

Current research indicates that a maintenance level stretch should be no shorter than ten seconds, while a stretch to increase range of motion must be held for thirty seconds or more. When stretching, be aware of the line of the stretch and the muscle groups being stretched. Don't strain. Often, as you stretch one side of the body, the other side contracts. In order to stretch most effectively, your attention should always be on lengthening the side of the body that's stretching. You don't want to contract the opposite side muscularly, because this can lead to compression in the tissue. Stretching both limbers the body and strengthens the tendons and ligaments. The wondrous body strengthens these connective tissues in response to persistent, nondamaging stress.

Side Stretch

Taking a wide stable stance, reach the right arm vertically, allowing the left hand to fall toward the foot. Bend the head and torso to the left to allow the right side to maximally lengthen from the foot out to the fingertips. If you go past vertical with this stretch, support the weight of the left side by putting your left palm on your leg. Repeat on the opposite side.

Side Stretch

Neck Stretch

The neck is quite fragile, so you want to stretch it gently. Stretch your right ear up to the sky, lengthening along the line of your neck. Do not contract the side opposite the stretch by trying to get the ear to the shoulder, because this can compress your neck! Repeat on the left side.

Neck Stretch 1

Hang the weight of your left arm on your right shoulder and stretch the right side again. Repeat on the left side.

Neck Stretch 2

Sun Salutation

The essentials of the Sun Salutation are borrowed from yoga, although this version has some additions. It is a very thorough stretching routine. Breathe deeply and comfortably throughout, holding each position for a minimum of ten seconds.

Stretch Up

Start with the feet together and stretch your arms above your head. Feel the stretch from the soles of your feet to your fingertips.

Stretch Up

Bend at Hips

Place your hands behind your lower back and bend at your hips. Don't curl your lower back. Keep your back straight to put the stretch in the hips and down the backs of your legs.

Bend at Hips

Left Leg Back

Step the left leg back into a long lunge, using your hands flat on the ground to support the transition. Rest the back of your left foot and lower leg on the floor with your right knee deeply bent. The first level of this stretch is with both hands on the ground extending from your rear foot through your head and front knee. If that's comfortable, try pressing the groin more toward the front heel, making the torso more upright and putting one hand on the forward knee.

Left Leg Back 1

If this is comfortable, you can increase the challenge of this stretch by raising first one hand and then both over your head.

Left Leg Back 2

Right Leg Back

Drop both hands to the floor and step the right foot back to join the left. Put both feet on the balls and arch the body up with the buttocks the highest part. Only the hands and feet are on the ground. Feel the stretch along the backs of your legs and Achilles tendons. Push against your arms to modulate the stretch to an intensity that's right for you.

Right Leg Back

Shift the weight out of one foot and stretch the other leg more deeply. Repeat on the other side.

Diving Push-Up

With both feet back on the floor, bend your arms to bring your nose forward and down between your hands.

Diving Push-Up 1

Continue the movement, arching up through the torso until your arms are straight again and your knees are touching the ground. The tops of your feet are on the ground, and you should feel an arching stretch through the front of the torso and chest. Continue the line of extension through the crown of your head, tucking your chin a little. This will prevent compression in the back of your neck.

Diving Push-Up 2

Back on the Heels

Bending your knees, move your pelvis back until you're sitting on your heels. Allow your forehead to rest on the ground. Keep your arms extended in front with your palms down and stretch out your fingers. Breathe deeply and feel the expansion in your lower back.

Back on the Heels

Left Leg Forward

Come up onto your hands and knees and swing your left leg forward into a lunge. Keep the back of the right foot and lower leg on the floor and the left knee deeply bent. The first level of this stretch is with both hands on the ground extending from the rear foot through the head and front knee. If that is comfortable, try pressing the groin more toward the front heel, making the torso more upright and putting one hand on the forward knee. If that is comfortable, you can increase the challenge of this stretch by raising first one hand and then both over the head.

Left Leg Forward

Turn for Adductors

Keeping the weight in your left leg, turn to the side and stretch the muscles of the inside of your right leg. Your left foot can be resting on a toe or flat on the ground—you may even prefer to rest on your left knee. Use your hands on the ground to help balance. Repeat on the other side.

Turn for Adductors 1

If you like, you can do both sides at once as a split. Make sure you support yourself with your hands on the ground. However you do this stretch, be gentle and don't strain.

Turn for Adductors 2

Hamstrings

Sinking one knee to the ground, extend your other leg out in front of you, with your heel on the ground. Straighten your leg and fold at the hip joint to stretch the hamstring muscles of the back of the leg. Keep your spine mostly straight; don't curl your lower back. If you like, grab your foot with one hand and put your other hand on your knee.

Hamstrings

You can increase the stretch by pulling one foot while you use the other to stabilize your body and help the bend stay in the hip joint and not in the lower back. After a minimum of ten seconds, drop your other knee to the floor and switch sides.

Bend at Hips

Bring your feet together and stand up, bending once more at the hips with your hands behind your lower back. Don't curl your lower back. Keep your back straight to put the stretch in the hips and down the backs of your legs.

Bend at Hips

Stretch Up

Bend your knees and push through the soles of your feet to straighten up, and then stretch your arms above your head. Feel the stretch from the soles of your feet to your fingertips.

Stretch Up

Stretch One Side

Reach one arm up a bit further than the other, shifting your weight into the opposite side. Repeat on the other side.

Stretch One Side

Hands Behind the Lower Back Arching

Place your hands behind your lower back and pelvis and arch up, looking at the sky. After ten seconds, bend your knees and push through your feet to stand erect.

Hands Behind the Lower Back Arching

Ankles

Most ankle injuries occur to the ligaments and tendons on the outside of the ankle. By stretching this side, you can strengthen this tissue. If you've had an ankle injury in the past, be gentle and use this stretch as an opportunity to more deeply feel the current condition of your ankle. Be gentle and careful.

To do the stretch, put your weight on one leg and put your other foot on the outer edge of your foot. Put weight into the ankle in a controlled fashion, giving your ankle a comfortable stretch. If you want, hold on to a chair, table, or wall to further stabilize your balance.

Ankles

CHAPTER 7

BASIC STANCES

Read through this chapter and familiarize yourself with the basics (relating to relaxation, posture, and so on) before you try movements beyond warm-ups. In these stances you are seeking to create a stable platform from the pelvis down—a platform upon which the upper body can rest. After the platform is created, you use your breath to generate a sense of spaciousness and lift in the upper body. The breath is full and deep into the lower abdomen, your shoulders rest on the rib cage, and your neck is free to allow the head to float. Your chin is slightly dropped, your tongue touches the roof of your mouth lightly (to relax the lower jaw), and your head floats as if it were suspended from the crown.

Feet, Legs, and Pelvis Shape

This exercise is a critically important aspect of posture. It is only when you have a solid structure from the pelvis down through your feet that you can really feel comfortable and allow your energy to flow. This structure is common in many martial arts. The general requirements of Feet, Legs, and Pelvis Shape apply to all the stances.

The weakest point of the leg is typically the knee. As a consequence, the structural requirements of the knee dictate the way you use your legs. The knee is a hinge joint, and as with metal hinges, if the hinge is twisted as it opens and closes it will eventually break. So pay precise attention to keeping the bones of the upper and lower legs in line so that the knee is not twisted.

Correct placement

If the forward knee is twisted, the big toe of the forward foot peels off the ground. To avoid this, make sure your navel points in the same direction as your weighted thigh, knee, and foot.

When your weight is back, your rear knee may want to twist in. To prevent this, keep your navel pointed in the same direction as the weighted thigh, knee, and foot.

Protecting your knee joints requires that you spread or round your crotch so that rather than feeling as though your legs meet in the pelvis as an upside-down V, you feel them meeting as an upside-down U. If you do this and keep your feet at the width of your pelvis, your leg bones will be in alignment and your knees and ankles should feel comfortable.

After you're in this shape, you want to brace your legs slightly as if you're on the deck of a ship that's moving with the waves. By bracing slightly in the legs, you will feel more solid. Bracing corrects the problem shown in the following image, where the weight is forward and the rear knee is collapsed.

The weight is forward and the rear knee is collapsed.
In this collapsed stance, the little toe will start to roll
off the ground, and you'll feel weak.

In order to have a clear experience of the stance you're cultivating, go ahead and do it wrong on purpose as illustrated here so that you will have a clear experience of what you want to avoid.

50/50 Posture

Place your feet parallel and shoulder-width apart.

50/50 Posture

Your ankle, knee, and hip joints should be slightly flexed and springy, and your crotch should be slightly rounded to bring your knees over your feet and to create a slight sense of being braced. Your posture is similar to sitting slightly on a high stool.

70/30 Posture

In this posture you have taken a step forward, maintaining your width and turning the rear foot out slightly on your heel. Your weight is 70 percent forward (hence the name of this posture), with the forward knee above the toe. Your navel points forward in the same direction as your front foot, while your rear foot is turned out at a 45-degree angle. Your ankle, knee, and hip joints should be slightly flexed and springy, and your crotch should be slightly rounded to bring the knees over the feet and to create a slight sense of being braced. In taking your step forward, you have to sit a little lower on your high stool. In more advanced practice with this posture, make sure that your heel, big toe, and little toe of each foot are on the floor and that 70 percent of your weight is in the balls of your feet.

70/30 Posture

100 Percent Back

For this posture, you don't move the feet from the 70/30, but simply move the weight back above the rear foot. You should maintain a firm, flat contact between the front foot and the floor. When you're back, your navel points in the same direction as your rear foot. Your ankle, knee, and hip joints should be slightly flexed and springy, and your crotch should be slightly rounded to bring your knees over your feet and to create a slight sense of being braced.

100 Percent Back

Empty Foot on Heel

In tai chi you call a weighted foot "full" and an unweighted foot "empty" or "hollow." In this stance all the weight is on one foot and the heel of the empty foot lightly touches the floor. Generally this stance is used in preparation to draw back the unweighted leg. Because all the weight is on one leg, you attend to the structural requirements of that leg, assuring that the upper and lower leg aren't twisted relative to each other so that the hinge joint of the knee can remain springy. Similarly, you don't "cock" out the weighted hip, because this tends to lock the joint, removing its springy quality. Your navel points in the same direction as your weighted foot and knee. Your empty leg is kept loose with all the joints unlocked and your knee bent. The line of your empty foot (drawn from mid-ball to mid-heel) runs a little to the outside of your weighted heel. Even in this stance (and in the next single-weighted stance) you should feel a springy sense of being braced.

Empty Foot on Heel

Empty Foot on Toe

This stance is commonly called a "cat stance" in the martial arts, and it is used to free the empty foot for a kick. Because all your weight is in one leg, you first attend to the structural requirements of that leg, assuring that the upper and lower leg aren't twisted relative to each other so that the hinge joint of the knee can remain springy. Similarly, you don't "cock" out the weighted hip, because this tends to lock the joint, removing its springy quality. Your navel points in the same direction as your weighted foot and knee. Your empty leg is kept loose with all the joints unlocked and your knee bent. The line of your empty foot (drawn from mid-ball to mid-heel) runs into your weighted heel. Maintain the springy sense of being braced. Keep the line of your lower leg vertical; don't draw your empty foot back too close to the weighted foot, because this impedes the freedom of your leg to kick.

Empty Foot on Toe

Stepping

In tai chi stepping, you want to maintain balance at all times and step lightly like a cat. In the following stepping drills, keep your feet shoulder-width apart.

You start with a 70/30 Posture with your weight forward. In order to step, you first must turn your front foot out slightly on the heel.

On rougher surfaces this will require you to shift some of your weight back; on smoother surfaces you may be able to simply lift the ball of the foot and pivot out on the heel.

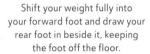

Shift your weight fully into your forward foot and draw your rear foot in beside it, keeping the foot off the floor.

Reach out forward and a bit to the side (to reestablish width) with that foot, heel touching first, and place the full foot down without shifting your weight into it. Now you should be in a 100 Percent Back stance.

Then, by pushing through your new rear leg,
shift your weight 70 percent forward, and you're
ready to repeat the process on the other side.

Because you're stepping from one 70/30 Posture into the next, you're going from a shoulder-width stance to a 100 Percent Back stance to the next 70/30. As you move through the changes of weight and position, you must continue to protect your knees by ensuring that your pelvis adjusts to keep the bones of your thigh and lower leg in line with your weighted leg.

When you're ready to integrate the breath with your stepping, inhale as you draw to the center and exhale as you step and shift forward.

90 Degrees Stepping

Often, you need to adjust your stance to face a new challenge. This step teaches you how to step in strongly at 90 degrees.

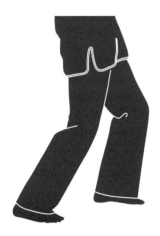 

Start with a 70/30 Posture facing north, with your weight forward on the left leg.

Shift fully into your forward leg, drawing your right leg in beside your left leg.

Turning your gaze 90 degrees to the east, step east and to the side (for width) on your heel, rolling your foot down flat with no weight.

Then, by pushing out of your heel of your rear foot, shift the weight 70 percent forward.

Pay attention at this point to ensure that you don't turn in on your toe, nor that you collapse your rear knee. If you have a tendency to want to pivot on the ball of your foot, usually you're stepping too narrowly. If you draw a line forward from the center of your rear heel that's parallel with the line of your forward foot, the lines should be shoulder-width apart.

The mechanics of the 90 Degrees Stepping drill can be adopted to a 135 Degrees Stepping drill for a more advanced exercise.

CHAPTER 8

HAND AND ARM POSTURES

The requirements of hand and arm postures reflect the two concerns of energy flow and effective body mechanics. You will develop wonderful coordination and grace using these postures.

Beautiful Lady's Wrist

Beautiful Lady's Wrist refers to a postural requirement emphasized by Cheng Man-Ching, a famed modern master of tai chi, that is often not stressed in other schools of tai chi. This term simply refers to holding your wrist in an open position so that your energy is free to flow into your palms.

Beautiful Lady's Wrist

Palms Resting on Pillow of Air

When one or both arms are at your sides, they must remain alive and not become limp. An alive arm at rest has a slight forward curve at the elbow and wrist, almost as if the arm is resting on an updraft of air. This is called having the palm resting on a pillow of air.

Palms Resting on Pillow of Air

Shoulder Down to Elbow Up to Wrist

This is a general rule for arm structure in which you keep the elbows down and weighted in order to ensure that the shoulder blades remain attached to the latissimus dorsi muscles (shoulder muscles of the back) and, thus, to the rib cage and your body as a whole.

Dealing with Blocked Energy

Most of us have habitual tension patterns that show up as pain and blocked energy when we simply stand still. Working with this area will help you understand and release the blocked energy, but be patient and compassionate with yourself.

Holding the Ball

This posture is often used in tai chi as a transitional movement. It provides a good opportunity for you to reconnect with your sense of energy between your palms. The energy ball that's held is generally the size of a large beach ball. If vertical, the lower hand is at the level of the navel while the upper hand is at the level of the collarbone. This posture has a myriad of defensive and offensive applications.

Holding the Ball

Ward Off

This posture uses either or both arms. Your arm(s) are in an arc in front of your body with your palm(s) facing the center line at about the level of the base of the sternum. Your arm(s) follow the Shoulder Down to Elbow Up to Wrist rule. This posture is used as an extra layer of protection between you and the incoming energy. It can also be used as a posture to attack with your forearm.

Ward Off

Ward Off is a central energy in tai chi and should be present in all your movements. Think of it as the energy inside an inflated balloon or the energy you adopt when pushing through a crowd. You literally expand your body into a more resilient structure. Having braced your legs, you then extend your arms and the torso with a pushing energy (known as Peng energy) to create an even more stable and resilient structure.

Two-Handed Push

In this posture you position yourself as if you were pushing a vehicle out of a ditch. Your arms follow the Shoulder Down to Elbow Up to Wrist rule, and your palms face away from your body as wide as your shoulders, with your fingertips no higher than your shoulders. You use Beautiful Lady's Wrist, although in application your hands would conform with the object being pushed.

Two-Handed Push

One-Handed Push

This posture is the same as the Two-Handed Push method except that you use only one hand. As a consequence, the pushing hand must move closer to the midline in order to maintain power. The first knuckle of the thumb tends to be on the midline.

One-Handed Push

Hook Hand

This is a signature hand position for tai chi. Here, the tips of the fingers all touch the tip of the thumb. The hand then hangs lightly from the wrist. This consolidates the strength of the fingers into a single "beak." In some martial arts applications, this hand position is also used to signify a grab with that hand.

Hook Hand

Fist

With the fingers closed and the thumb curled down and over them, the Fist position is held lightly. There is a little space within the fist itself. Imagine that you've captured a tiny fairy: don't squeeze and crush the fairy. In a martial arts application, however, the fist is tightened just before the point of impact.

Fist

Stress and Chi

A stressed body is not a relaxed body, which is hardly a surprise. But also a tense body can't take in its full amount of breath/chi, and that's a big problem. The body is stressing, responding to all the bouncing thoughts and feelings. Yet this is the scattered state in which most people live. Do your best to remember your breathing while you practice.

Moving On to the Yang Style Short Form

The series of movements (or form) that you can learn next is called the Yang Style short form, abridged by Cheng Man-Ching. Professor Cheng (following the Chinese pattern, the surname is first) was a highly respected tai chi master, as well as a master of calligraphy, painting, and traditional Chinese medicine (TCM). He was one of the first tai chi masters to teach tai chi to non-Chinese in the United States. Finding Americans to be a rather impatient people, he shortened the form to fit more easily with our hurried lifestyles. He took the traditional Yang Style, which is said to have 108 movements, and removed the repetitions to create his shortened form. Once you master the basic postures and poses in this book, you may want to continue your tai chi practice and learn the Yang Style short form. See the Resources list at the end of this book for other recommended books and websites.

CHAPTER 9

CONTINUING YOUR PRACTICE

Now that you've gotten started with tai chi, you may need help in finding ways to continue practicing on a regular basis. This chapter will provide you with some tips.

PRACTICING TAI CHI REGULARLY

Be consistent in how much time you dedicate each day to each practice. Show up at about the same time each day. This practice of integrating tai chi into your life will create a body habit, and you'll be able to treat yourself to chi breaks and mini vacations at the drop of a hat.

Body habits are powerful. Your life is probably much more influenced by them than you realize:

* It is often a body habit that makes something feel right.
* It is a body habit that takes food and turns it into nourishment.
* It is body habit that allows muscles long unused to build up quickly when exercised years later.

Your body's habits push you into action. If you are looking to replace troubling body habits (overeating, excess shoulder tension, nervous habits) with useful body habits, habits that lend themselves to an improving inner and outer life, then tai chi is a great idea.

Be Patient

It takes six weeks of steady commitment to form a body habit. This is because you're altering the nervous system. The nervous system thrives on variety. Creating a new body habit asks the nervous system to liven up its wiring by telling the muscles to do something a little different. The nervous system then helps memory store the movement into the muscle. This can take a while and depends heavily on the person. In general, younger people are able to train their nervous system faster than older people.

Most people become programmed in their movements. In some ways, this is great because it creates predictable walking, sitting, stepping, and so on. The downside is that some muscles get overused and others are chronically underused. This creates movement stiffness and balance problems. The other problem is the nervous system isn't receiving what it loves—new, pleasant stimulation via tai chi!

Look Forward to It

Whenever something tedious, irritating, disappointing, tiring, and so on happens, say to yourself, "I can hardly wait to do tai chi," "Thank goodness I'll be able to practice tai chi tonight," "I'll definitely feel better after tai chi," or "When this is over, I can practice tai chi!"

Tai Chi Does Not Have "Belts"

Tai chi doesn't have belts, like some other martial arts practices, but according to instructor Gene Burnett, there are four interconnected levels of work in tai chi:

- The bone level: Fundamental principles.
- The muscle level: Relaxation.
- The energy level: A deeper energetic connection.
- The spiritual level: Surrendering ego-control and identification.

Use Your Practice to Put Off a Habit

Suppose you have a habit that you want to have less of a hold on you or one you would like to break. Use tai chi to break those habits. For example: "I will have that ice cream after I finish my tai chi," "I'll watch that next episode, but first I want to do tai chi," "I'll check my phone after I have enjoyed my tai chi," or "I'm going to put off worrying about such-and-such while I do my tai chi."

BEING CONSISTENT

Because the first six weeks are the hardest to make the time, be consistent. You have to make the effort to really do it, not just go through the motions. Life is so busy that you may be challenged to fit in one more activity, or you may lack sustained interest. Or, perhaps, a last-minute change of plans keeps you from practicing. But if you continue to plod along taking tai chi space no matter what, time will begin to assist you. You will find that it gets easier and easier to have the time. Life will be more enjoyable, your health will improve, and a quiet state of mind will settle in.

By doing the movements at a regular time (morning, midday, or evening) your body will develop the habit of putting down the built-up muscular tension. It is like setting down a heavy load you've been carrying all day and then letting your muscles rest. This relaxation settles into your body as you practice. Your mind slides into your movements. You have great relief from not thinking about the past, the future, or an imagined parallel present. The flowing breathing settles in. This occurs even if you know only a few positions. Put your whole self into them. Do what you know, repeat them in a flowing cycle. Settle down in the moment.

As you become consistent, your practice becomes a familiar body-mind memory for you. This memory strengthens over time from regular practice. A state of increasing relaxation seeps more and more into routine daily moments. You will find eventually that you're able to make a choice about how much tension you want to feel in any given event. Someone is rude, and you start to react, but a relaxed response has now become a part of your life. It is right there for you to draw from. You let the person's behavior roll right by you. You choose your own reaction. You're not controlled by stress responses that have built up over time. Life seems sweeter and happier. Your chi smooths out and improves.

Tai Chi Brings Relaxation

Through your practice, you will be more relaxed. Not couch-potato relaxed, but just truly relaxed, the way you'd like to feel all the time. When you commit to a regular practice session, you halt the buildup of tension your busy life creates in your muscles.

Time may also seem more spacious. In a world of multitasking and many activities drawing on you all at once, this sensation can feel like a miracle. Instead of the day feeling tightly wound around you, you have a feeling of spaciousness. Everyone else may still be feeling rushed, pressured, and harried. You, however, are feeling a bit more leisurely, a bit more confident that everything is in its right place. You may find that instead of running down a tunnel of stressed and focused thoughts, you now are aware of more of the world around you. It is the classic "take time to smell the roses."

TAKING TAI CHI BREAKS

One way to slow down is to take tai chi breaks wherever you are. Learning the movement and combining the breath and then engaging the mind are a perfect menu for refreshing and stimulating rest and relaxation. The ongoing mastery of the breath and the movements call forth ever-increasing sensitivity that's required to continue to improve the movement. The type of sensitivity that tai chi calls forth stimulates the nervous system, heightens it, and then feeds it with full and healthy chi. This, then, provides a wonderful combination for soothing stimulation. The art of having tai chi breaks becomes as natural as breathing.

You will find that simple snippets of tai chi occur to you during your day, as illustrated in the following examples.

Waiting in Line

While waiting in line somewhere you may find yourself shifting your weight slightly, moving the weight from being primarily on one leg and then the other. As you shift the weight, you will be experiencing tai chi's full and empty, or yang and yin, teachings. As you gently shift the weight to one leg you can feel it fill, like a pitcher being filled with fluid, while your other leg is now empty and very light. Slowly, the weight can shift over. The full leg now loses its fullness to the empty leg. The previously empty leg is now full and deeply rooted in the ground. The line moves forward, and you move the empty leg first. You feel the firm rootedness of the full leg. You let the fullness pour into the empty leg that just changed position. This now full leg roots to the ground, and the newly empty leg moves forward. You can repeat this through the whole line.

Several great things have happened here. You've brought your busy, busy mind into the present. Your relaxed muscle memory of tai chi has taken over the rest of your body. Your breath has deepened and become more normal. You've just spent five minutes in line and it has passed in a moment—a very constructive moment: a mini vacation.

Sitting in Traffic

Or you may be sitting in traffic. It may seem as if every person on the road is in collusion in trying to get in your way. You really need to relax and just let it be crowded, but how? Try reverse breathing (see Chapter 1). It renews your energy level, focuses and calms your mind, and makes you more accepting of this inconvenience. I wouldn't recommend doing any form of tai chi when actually moving in your car, because it could distract you at a critical moment, so do your reverse breath in the car only when you're stationary.

Enjoy the Everyday

Practicing tai chi is a way to embrace mindfulness and find pleasure in everyday moments. A relaxed person is naturally a more expanded person. A relaxed person appreciates more, enjoys giving more, receives with love, and sees more opportunities to enjoy still more.

Driving does provide a perplexing problem. You may have to drive many hours a day, so being able to center and calm yourself while driving is of great value. What I suggest trying is a brief exercise before you enter the car. Form a habit or ritual. Before you get into your car, while you're actually walking toward it, relax your tan t'ien. Your belly will relax out a bit. Let a breath flow into you and then back out. Feel your shoulders relax down. Draw another breath and release it. Now imagine the air is breathing you. Your body is open and relaxed, and the air falls into you and now flows out. And now you're at your car, more centered and prepared for anything that comes your way.

MAKING A COMMITMENT TO AN EXPANDED LIFE

Make a commitment to expand your awareness beyond your own self-contained life. There are endless distractions and responsibilities in daily life, but you can always find time to expand your view of the moment to include more. A flower, a baby's smile, something funny, a great piece of music, a great memory are just a few gifts that await you if you include more mindfulness in your life.

If you become overwhelmed, use tai chi to still your thoughts and expand your awareness. Are your kids driving you nuts at times, the noise, the busyness, the defiance—whatever? Put your fingers on your tan t'ien. Sink your breath to this point. Hold it for a second and exhale by releasing all the tension that is containing the inhale. Pull on your ears from top to lobes. Let your arms float up on an inhale, cross your arms over your chest, and place your hands on your neck. Take a literal step back and release your breath. Float your arms to your sides. You will feel more contained and ready to lay down boundaries that make sense for you and for them. Or you will be in a better position to turn tail and run to the nearest quiet space for a break!

Kids Can Practice Too!

The value of tai chi is the same for children as for anyone (see Chapters 1, 2, and 3), but it is a rare child who will want to learn the traditional form. Now, however, it is adapted in a way that children can learn to improve their balance, increase their coordination, improve interaction skills, and discover energetic sensitivity. For naturally energetically sensitive children, it can be very worthwhile to have those gentle but powerful sensitivities validated and learn to utilize them. Look for a child-focused class near you for a practice that will better engage little ones.

RESOURCES

BOOKS

The Complete Book of T'ai Chi by Stewart McFarlane and Tan Mew Hong

The Complete Book of Tai Chi Chuan: A Comprehensive Guide to the Principles and Practice by Wong Kiew Kit

Tai Chi Chuan Classical Yang Style: The Complete Long Form and Qigong by Yang Jwing-Ming

The Tao of Tai-Chi Chuan: Way to Rejuvenation by Jou Tsung Hwa

WEBSITES

Chen Style Tai Chi
www.chentaichi.com

Easy Tai Chi
www.easytaichi.com

International Yang Family Tai Chi Chuan Association
www.yangfamilytaichi.com

National Institutes of Health's National Center for Complementary and Integrative Health's Tai Chi and Qi Gong: In Depth
https://nccih.nih.gov/health/taichi/introduction.htm

Natural Cave's Beginner's Guide to Modern Tai Chi
http://naturalcave.com/posts/a-beginners-guide-to-modern-tai-chi

The Tai Chi Site
www.thetaichisite.com

Tai Chi Productions
www.taichiproductions.com

Taoist Tai Chi Society of the USA
www.taoist.org/usa

Wu Style Form Tai Ji Quan
www.wfdesign.com/tc

INDEX

50/50 Posture, 122
70/30 Posture, 123
90 Degrees Stepping, 130–31
100 Percent Back Posture, 124

Acupressure, 51, 57
Acupuncture, 51, 57
Aggression, 68
Aging process, 26, 38, 40–41, 44–47
Air quality, 62
Ankle stretch, 116
Ankle Swirls warm-up, 91
Ankles, relaxing, 68–69
Arm postures, 133–43. *See also* Postures
Arms, relaxing, 68–69
Attitude, 11, 50, 57, 74–76
Audiovisual equipment, 63

Back on Heels stretch, 107
Balance
    achieving, 30–31, 46–55, 79, 145–52
    flexibility and, 25–29
    improving, 17–19, 23–25
    relaxation and, 29–34, 79, 145–52
    stiffness and, 26, 147
    stress relief and, 19, 29–34, 38
    of yin and yang, 12, 36–37, 46–55, 150
Beautiful Lady's Wrist posture, 134

Bend at Hips stretch, 102, 112
Blood pressure, 27
Body, readying, 67–69
Body benefits
    balance, 17–19, 23–25
    blood pressure, 27
    body-soul harmony, 40–41, 45
    coordination, 17, 23–25
    flexibility, 14, 25–29, 64, 81
    migraine relief, 28
    mind-body harmony, 31, 37–39, 43–45, 64–65
    muscle tone, 9, 26–29
    skin tone, 26–27
Body habits, 146–51
Breaks, 67, 146, 149–51
Breathing
    air quality and, 62
    checklist for, 23
    circular breathing, 64–65
    for directing chi, 21–25, 50–51, 57, 80
    effective breathing, 17–23
    exercises for, 18–21, 62
    meditation and, 32, 35–38, 44
    organs and, 18–23, 27, 50–57
    proper breathing, 20–23
    relaxation and, 18–26
    reverse breathing, 20–23
    stress relief and, 19, 142
    toxins and, 62
    vitality and, 18–20
Burnett, Gene, 147

Cat Stance, 126
Centering technique, 10, 20, 44, 80, 151
Changquan, 11
Chen Ling Xi, 12
Chen Style, 13
Chen Wang Ting, 13
Cheng Man-Ching, 134, 143
Chi
    balancing, 46–55
    directing, 21–25, 50–51, 57, 80
    meridian system and, 46–51, 57, 65–66
    stress relief and, 19, 142
Children, 152
Chinese medicine, 51, 55–56, 143
Clarity, 11, 34–36, 44, 76
Classes, 69–74
Closeness, mutual, 52–53
Clothing, 24, 63–64
Commitment, 72–73, 151–52
Concentration, 31–33, 64–65, 78
Consistency, 145–52
Coordination, 17, 23–25, 64–65, 72, 80, 133
Creation, mutual, 52–53
Cross Crawl warm-up, 82
Cross Crawl with Twist warm-up, 83
Cycle of creation, 52–53
Cycle of life, 48, 56

Decay, 46
Decline, 46
Depression, relieving, 34
Destruction, mutual, 52, 54
Discipline, 72
Diving Push-Up stretch, 106

Earthly energies, 49
Elbow Massage warm-up, 92–93

Elements, 51–57
Emptiness concept, 18, 31, 35–36, 40–41, 79
Empty Foot on Heel stance, 125
Empty Foot on Toe stance, 126
Energy. *See also* Chi
    blocked energy, 136
    earthly energies, 49
    energy centers, 25, 65
    energy flow, 14, 46, 49–57
    heavenly energies, 49
    life force and, 18, 46
    meridian system and, 46–51, 57, 65–66
    positive energy, 50–51
    sleep and, 20
    vitality and, 18–20, 38, 46, 49
    yin and yang and, 14, 46, 49–57
Enlightenment, 32
Evenness concept, 31, 79

Fear, mutual, 52, 54
Feet, Legs, and Pelvis Shape stance, 118–21
Fist posture, 142
Flexibility, 14, 25–29, 64, 81
Focus, improving, 30–33, 38–40, 49, 64–65
Foot Figure Eight warm-up, 88–89
Fullness concept, 18, 31, 35–36, 41, 79

Grace, 23–25, 64–65, 79, 133
Green tea, 68
Growth, 40–41, 46, 65

Habits, forming, 146–51
Hamstring stretch, 111
Hand postures, 133–43. *See also* Postures
Hands, relaxing, 68–69

Hands Behind Lower Back Arching
    stretch, 115
Harmony, 11, 31–41, 43–50, 64–65
Headache relief, 28
Health
    aging process and, 26, 38,
        40–41, 44–47
    illness and, 40–41, 46–47, 55–57
    improving, 9–14
    maintaining, 41, 46, 55–57,
        148–51
    of organs, 18–23, 27, 50–57
    vitality and, 18–20, 38, 46, 49
Heavenly energies, 49
Herbal remedies, 57
Holding the Ball posture, 137
Hook Hand posture, 141
Hula Pelvis warm-up, 87
Hypertension, 27

I Ching, 9, 12, 44
Illness, 40–41, 46–47, 55–57
Incline, 46
Infinity Arms warm-up, 84–85
Inner life, 40–41, 46
Inner peace, 10–11, 14, 40, 78
Instructors. *See* Teachers
Intent, 21, 47, 66
Internal force, 48–49
Issues, troubleshooting, 77–79

Jewelry, 69
Joint flexibility, 26–29

Lao Tzu, 9
Left Leg Back stretch, 103–4
Left Leg Forward stretch, 108
Li Dao Zi, 11
Life, cycle of, 48, 56
Life force, 18, 46
Light, natural, 63

Long Fist, 11–12
Lotions, 68

Mantra yoga, 32
Mantras, 32–33
Martial arts
    levels of, 147
    stances for, 117–31, 142
    tai chi and, 10–13, 23–24, 48,
        55, 74–76
Meals, 41, 68
Meditation
    benefits of, 30–33, 35–38, 44,
        47, 57
    breathing and, 32, 35–38, 44
    everyday meditation, 38
    mantras for, 32–33
    moving meditation, 22, 30–33,
        80
    music for, 32, 57
    principles of, 31
    techniques for, 30–33
Memory, 19, 71, 148–52
Mental clarity, 11, 34–36, 44, 76
Meridian system, 46–51, 57, 65–66
Migraine relief, 28
Mind, readying, 64–67
Mind benefits
    body-mind harmony, 31, 37–39,
        43–45, 64–65
    body-soul harmony, 40–41,
        45–50
    concentration, 31–33, 64–65
    depression relief, 34
    focus, 30–33, 38–40, 49, 64–65
    meditation, 30–33, 35–38, 44,
        47, 57
    mental clarity, 11, 34–36, 44, 76
    quieting mind, 30, 34, 79
    slowing down, 36–38
    stress relief, 29–34, 38–41

Mindfulness, 34–40, 64–65, 151–52
Mini vacations, 67, 146
Movement philosophy, 14
Moving meditation, 22, 30–33, 80
Muscle memory, 19, 71, 150
Muscle tone, 9, 26–29
Music, 32, 57, 63
Mutual closeness, 52–53
Mutual creation, 52–53
Mutual destruction, 52, 54
Mutual fear, 52, 54

Nature connections, 51–57
Nature sounds, 63
Neck Stretch, 99–100
Nothingness, 14, 18, 45–46

One-Handed Push posture, 140
Oneness, 9–10, 14, 34, 45, 51–54
Organs, 18–23, 27, 50–57

Palms Resting on Pillow of Air
     posture, 135
Patience, 37, 136, 146–47
Peacefulness, 10–11, 14, 40, 78
Plié warm-up, 94–95
Positive attitude, 11, 50, 57, 74–76
Positive energy, 50–51
Postures
     50/50 Posture, 122
     70/30 Posture, 123
     90 Degrees Stepping, 130–31
     100 Percent Back, 124
     arm postures, 133–43
     Beautiful Lady's Wrist, 134
     Cat Stance, 126
     Empty Foot on Heel, 125
     Empty Foot on Toe, 126
     Feet, Legs, and Pelvis Shape,
          118–21
     Fist, 142

     hand postures, 133–43
     Holding the Ball, 137
     Hook Hand, 141
     improving, 28
     One-Handed Push, 140
     Palms Resting on Pillow of Air,
          135
     Shoulder Down to Elbow Up to
          Wrist, 136
     spine and, 18, 20, 28
     stances, 117–31, 133–43
     Stepping, 127–29
     Two-Handed Push, 139
     Ward Off, 138
Practice
     air quality for, 62
     attitude for, 74–76
     audiovisual equipment for, 63
     clothing for, 63–64
     commitment to, 72–73, 151–52
     concerns about, 77–79
     consistency with, 145–52
     discipline for, 72
     habits for, 146–51
     lighting for, 63
     mindfulness for, 34–40, 64–65,
          151–52
     music for, 63
     practice screens, 67
     preparing for, 61–79
     readying body for, 67–69
     readying mind for, 64–67
     space for, 62–63
     thankfulness for, 67
     time for, 14, 67–68, 78, 145–48
Prayer, 33. *See also* Meditation
Pregnancy, 27
Principles, 79–80
Push-Up stretch, 106

Quieting mind, 30, 34, 79

Relaxation
    achieving, 34–37, 79, 145–52
    balance and, 29–34, 79, 145–52
    breathing and, 18–26
    meditation and, 30–33
    practicing, 68–69
    stress relief and, 29–34, 38–41
Resiliency, 25, 37, 43–44, 57–58
Resources, 153–54
Reverse breathing, 20–23. See
    also Breathing
Right Leg Back stretch, 105
Rituals, 69, 151
Rooting concept, 31, 80

Safety, 26, 62, 66
Self-awareness, 38, 44–50, 56–57,
    65, 151–52
Self-protection, 23–24
Self-understanding, 54
Sexy Pelvis warm-up, 87
Shaolin Kungfu, 12
Shoulder Down to Elbow Up to
    Wrist posture, 136
Shoulder Rolls warm-up, 86
Side Stretch, 98
Sinking concept, 31, 80
Skin tone, 26–27
Sleep, 20, 37–38, 41, 58
Slowness concept, 36–38, 79
Societies, 153–54
Soul, 40–43, 45–50, 78
Source of all, 45–46
Space, creating, 62–63
Spiritual awareness, 38, 43–45, 78
Spiritual benefits, 43–58
Spiritual connection, 44–57
Spiritual growth, 49, 76
Spiritual light, 32
Spiritual wisdom, 40–41, 46–47,
    50, 74–76

Stances. See also Postures
    50/50 Posture, 122
    70/30 Posture, 123
    90 Degrees Stepping, 130–31
    100 Percent Back, 124
    Cat Stance, 126
    Empty Foot on Heel, 125
    Empty Foot on Toe, 126
    Feet, Legs, and Pelvis Shape, 118
    Stepping stance, 127–29
Stiffness, 26, 147
Stillness, 34, 45, 49
Stress relief, 19, 29–34, 38–41, 58
Stretch One Side, 114
Stretch Up, 101, 113
Stretches
    Ankles, 116
    Back on Heels, 107
    Bend at Hips, 102, 112
    Diving Push-Up, 106
    Hamstrings, 111
    Hands Behind Lower Back
        Arching, 115
    Left Leg Back, 103–4
    Left Leg Forward, 108
    Neck Stretch, 99–100
    Push-Up, 106
    Right Leg Back, 105
    Side Stretch, 98
    Stretch One Side, 114
    Stretch Up, 101, 113
    Sun Salutation, 101–15
    Turn for Adductors, 109–10
Sun Style, 13

Tai chi
    basics of, 59–152
    benefits of, 9, 15–58
    for body, 17–28, 67–69
    for children, 152
    classes on, 69–74

commitment to, 72–73, 151–52
concerns about, 77–79
consistency with, 145–52
costs for, 24
explanation of, 9–10, 14
instructors of, 69–74, 143, 147
levels of, 147
for mind, 29–41, 64–67
philosophy of, 9, 14, 32, 44, 73
postures, 117–31, 133–43
practicing, 61–80, 145–52
preparing for, 61–80
principles of, 79–80
resources for, 153–54
roots of, 11–13
safety precautions for, 26, 62, 66
space for, 62–63
for spirit, 43–58
stances, 117–31, 133–43
stretches, 97–116
warm-ups, 81–95
Tai chi chuan, 9–13
Tan t'ien
    balance and, 50–51
    breathing and, 19–25, 65, 80, 151
    chi and, 19–25, 30, 50, 69
    description of, 19–25
    energy center and, 25, 65
    posture and, 28
    relaxation and, 69, 151–52
Tao Te Ching, 9
Taoism, 9, 45
Tea, 35, 68
Teachers, 69–74, 143, 147
Technology, 56, 63, 67
Thankfulness, 67
Time for practice, 14, 67–68, 78, 145
Toxins, 62
Training, 12–13, 69–74
Traits, 54–55
Troubleshooting tips, 77–79

Turn for Adductors stretch, 109–10
Two-Handed Push posture, 139

Visualization, 32
Vitality, 18–20, 38, 46, 49. See
    also Energy

Wang Zong Yue, 13
Ward Off posture, 138
Warm-ups
    Ankle Swirls, 91
    Cross Crawl, 82
    Cross Crawl with Twist, 83
    Elbow Massage, 92–93
    Foot Figure Eight, 88–89
    Hula Pelvis, 87
    Infinity Arms, 84–85
    Plié, 94–95
    Sexy Pelvis, 87
    Shoulder Rolls, 86
    Wrist Swirls, 90
Wholeness, 14, 18, 45–46
Wisdom, 40–41, 44, 50, 74–76
Wrist Swirls warm-up, 90
Wrists, relaxing, 68–69
Wu chi, 14, 45–46
Wu Style, 13

Xu Xuan Ping, 11

Yang chi, 49
Yang flow, 46, 50
Yang Lu Chen, 13
Yang Style, 13, 143
Yeung, Albert, 34
Yin and yang, 9, 12–14, 18, 36–37,
    46–57, 150
Yin chi, 49
Yoga, 32, 33, 58, 101

Zhang San Feng, 12